SCHUBERT'S SONG TECHNIQUE

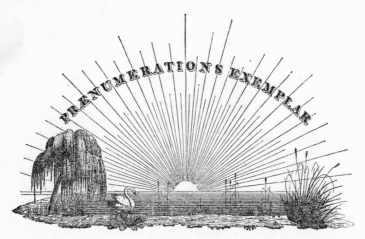

Two vignettes:

Above from the second edition of *Die schöne Müllerin* (after 1828).
Below from the first edition of *Schwanengesang* (1829).

SCHUBERT'S
SONG TECHNIQUE

Ernest G. Porter

LONDON: DENNIS DOBSON

© 1961 by Ernest G. Porter

First published in Great Britain in 1961 by

Dobson Books Ltd., 80 Kensington Church Street, London, W.8

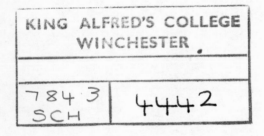
Set and printed in Great Britain by

Clarke, Doble & Brendon Ltd., Cattedown, Plymouth

CONTENTS

LIST OF ILLUSTRATIONS

All the illustrations are taken from *Franz Schubert, Sein Leben in Bildern* compiled by Otto Erich Deutsch (Georg Müller, 1913)

PREFACE

In a work of this dimension it is clearly not possible to make reference to every song of Schubert; nor indeed do I think it necessary. My aim is to show the character of his 'inspiration', and to emphasize, perhaps, that this sprang from intellectual foundations of which the casual listener seems often unaware. Of the principal musical examples a number are taken from some of the great songs which are unwarrantably neglected, yet which show Schubert's workmanship at its best and reveal his most intimate thoughts.

There are certain books indispensable to any writer on Schubert. These include the *Revisionsbericht* which contains the editorial notes on the complete edition of the songs, O. E. Deutsch's *Schubert Thematic Catalogue* and *Schubert: a documentary biography*, and Moritz Bauer's *Die Lieder Franz Schuberts*, *Schubert's Songs* by R. Capell, *Schubert* by Alfred Einstein, and *A Schubert Symposium* edited by Gerald Abraham.

Schubert by M. J. E. Brown was published after my manuscript was completed, but particular issues there raised are noted in occasional footnotes and in the details of Appendix I. Mr. Brown however, has most kindly read this book and made several suggestions for its improvement, while Dr. Young also proposed several amendments, and I gratefully acknowledge my debt to them both.

I have also to thank the editors of the *Music Quarterly, Music and Letters* and *Musical Opinion* for permission to use some of the material from my articles on *Schubert's Harmony, Schubert's Song Workshop, Schubert and the Major Third* and *Schubert's Expression Marks,* respectively.

Thanks are also due to J. M. Dent & Son for permission to quote from O. E. Deutsch's *Schubert: a documentary biography (Franz Schubert, Die Dokumente seines Lebens and Schaffens)* and to Dr. Deutsch himself for permission to reproduce the illustrations from the third volume *(Sein Leben in Bildem)* of the German edition.

Translations of quotations from the poems which have been used to illustrate details of expression are given in footnotes, but these are not necessary where a phrase is quoted mainly for the purpose of identification in the music. Many musical terms are not found in the smaller musical dictionaries and have therefore been included in Appendix II which has been prepared with the aid of Mr. Ernst Reinhold. For this and for the encouragement and advice he has given me over many years in my study and translation of Schubert's songs, I should like to express my sincere gratitude.

E. G. PORTER

EARLY PROGRESS

SCHUBERT'S revolution in the realm of song may be
likened to that of Wagner's in opera, but how much clear
and calculated reasoning went into the work we cannot
know. Genius appears to work so much by instinct that
we are sometimes inclined to think it needs nothing else,
but as a composition cannot be produced without fore-
thought and self-criticism the amount of intellectual
effort in a work of art must be commensurate with its
greatness. If it seems to have been produced with
astonishing facility that is only because of the immense
experience previously accumulated in experiment, and
continual practice in the art of expression.

Thus it is possible to follow the trend of Schubert's
theorizing by an examination of the songs, and discover
the reasoning that led to these works without having to
decide whether it was due to conscious processes of
thought or to an upsurge from the unconscious mind
aroused by constant rumination on the interpretation of
poetic expression in musical terms. It must be noted at
the outset that this examination is objective in nature
and cannot determine the real artistic value of the music.
This value is determined by the listener himself almost
regardless of the technique involved in the composition
of the music, consideration of which is an afterthought.

Hence we may analyse a great song and observe its salient features and intricacies of form and harmony; but such knowledge will not disclose its true power, which is the thought and emotion of its creator. His mind is revealed in the music, but to examine this music is but to examine the means of expression.

Nevertheless such investigation enables us to comprehend still further the beauty and even the power of a composition. To perceive the simplicity of material that produces such a song as 'Heidenröslein' or the abundance of technical ingenuity that goes to the making of some of the larger songs is to enrich our appreciation and heighten our enjoyment. Fortunately in the case of Schubert's songs there is no need to prove their greatness. It is only necessary to analyse the processes by which this greatness was achieved.

German poetry in the eighteenth century had risen to great heights, and many minor musicians had popularized the simple ballad and lyric. Their work was charming and their music had a fairly wide general appeal, but the great composers were too engrossed in the larger musical forms to add much to this rising mode of expression in which even the leading singers were beginning to take an interest. The time was therefore ripe for music to branch out in a fresh field of expression, and fortunately a young genius of fourteen with a gift of rich and significant melody had taken up song-writing in a tentative manner. The term is permissible because the young Schubert quite evidently set out to be a composer of orchestral, choral and chamber works. He lived in the midst of church and instrumental music and even at this early age played in an orchestra and at times conducted it. Such activity would naturally set his mind on producing similar works that could be performed by choir or orchestra or in the string quartet of his own family.

Of the first fifty numbers in the Deutsch Thematic Catalogue only eight are songs. But Schubert had a love of poetry and an irresistible desire to express in music the scenes and emotions it aroused in him, and we find that although he started in 1811[1] with four very long songs and then dropped to two in 1812, there were six in 1813, twenty-four in the following year, and nearly one hundred and fifty in 1815. During this period there were also a few Italian arias and unfinished song sketches which have not been included in these figures, but it seems clear that the urge to song-writing was a gradual development of a youthful attraction.

This comparatively slow approach was also probably due to the choice of poets. The Schubert family were musical rather than literary and there would not have been a wide range of reading matter available. No doubt some of Schubert's friends, so soon to become members of the famous Circle, being literary rather than musical, introduced much fresh poetry to him; and even provided him with their own poems much to the indignation of some of the modern critics. This explains why the early songs are confined to the older poets and to Schiller and Goethe whose works must have been in every home.

A poem can be set *in extenso,* in which case a strong

---

[1] We are of course limited to extant works. No doubt much was written in a tentative way before this year.

sense of form is necessary in order to attain unity, or in strophic form which entails careful consideration of suitability for such treatment. Schubert, quite naturally, at first had neither qualification. He commenced in the manner which he maintained to the end. He set any poem that attracted him regardless of the difficulties involved, and it is by these difficulties that we may trace his early development.

Most writers have referred to his predecessors in song-writing and have concentrated chiefly on Zumsteeg. Spaun wrote in 1829 that Schubert knew these songs as a boy which may have 'somewhat awakened his inclination to German song and incited his innate talent for that sort of composition to its first utterances':[1] and adds that in some of the earliest songs 'this influence may in fact perhaps be noticeable'. But even at that early time the writer confines himself to mere suggestions; and examination of the Zumsteeg songs proves that he was right to be cautious. There is indeed little connection and the influence, if any, is to be found in the shorter Zumsteeg songs which have a freedom of form alien to the classical school.

Zumsteeg (1760-1802) was highly esteemed by Haydn who was much distressed at his death. He was a friend of the poet Schiller, and was one of the several popular composers at that time. J. F. Reichardt (1752–1814) was much admired by Mendelssohn, especially for his choral works, and had much influence on Goethe, as had Zelter (1758–1832) who with Mendelssohn was largely responsible for the revival of Bach's works.

[1] O. E. Deutsch, *The Documents*, p. 877.

Another composer of this period was Schulz (1747–1800), and even if the works of these song-writers are now practically forgotten they performed a valuable service in bringing this form of music into the foreground, for although their compositions are technically far below the works of the great masters they infused a new spirit into music, breaking away from the classical approach and introducing simple well-phrased melodies which often expressed homely and unsophisticated sentiments.

Although Schubert cannot have been influenced to any extent by their technique he was no doubt caught up in the new stream of expression which covered a large range of new subject matter by making use of the already rich field of poetry, and as already suggested, he must have been influenced by Zumsteeg's individuality of expression.

Example 1 is a complete setting by Zumsteeg of Matthisson's 'An den Abendstern' (of three stanzas) in which there are four changes of time. It commences with a nice sense of phrasing to accent 'Liebe' and 'trübe' with rhyming cadences in tonic and relative minor. Then follows a modulation to the subdominant, a semi-recitative in the supertonic key and a final phrase in the opening key. This forms a tonal structure of A flat, F minor, D flat, B flat, and A flat, falling in thirds, which we shall see later became a typical Schubertian key relationship, as did the freedom of form in a much extended manner.

Some of Zumsteeg's more elaborate songs are as good as Schubert's, especially of the Matthisson poems such as 'Nachtgesang' and 'Geisternähe', and 'Thekla' (by

Ex. 1. An den Abendstern (Zumsteeg)

Schiller) is much better than Schubert's first setting; but although the harmonies are often very effective the accompaniments are undistinguished for they rarely get beyond simple arpeggio figures.

Schubert's accompaniments had from the first the utmost variety and he may have learned something from Mozart's songs. A glance at the latter's airs such as 'Dans un bois' and 'Oiseaux, si tous les ans', or songs such as 'Warnung', and 'Das Lied der Trennung' will disclose obvious similarities, while the accompaniment to 'Lied der Freiheit' looks like the prototype of the famous brook music. We may at least be certain that Schubert learned something from all the music he could get, but this was at quite an early age so integrated with his own personality that in the songs there is little opportunity of proving decisive links.

What no doubt is derived from Zumsteeg is the use of recitative in the song-form and as this occurs so often in the course of these early works it is necessary to consider its use and purpose. It is a usage difficult to define. Its proper place seems to be as a prelude to an aria, or as dialogue in the course of an opera. In the cantata-like songs with which Schubert commenced, recitative passages are recognized as such and do not seem out of place as they do in the normal form of song. In the former they provide declamatory sections and serve as a foil to the lyrical ones, but in the latter they appear incongruous. That Schubert had reason for adopting this method at first, and then turned its disadvantages to vital purpose we shall see later.

The difficulty, as mentioned above, is to define recitative as used in these songs. It is usual for the singer to claim great freedom as to time and rendering in such sections, but Schubert is in some cases precise. In 'Hagars Klage' there is an unaccompanied phrase marked *recit* followed a few bars later by *a tempo*. Later a similar passage has the latter sign but not the former. In 'Des Mädchens Klage' there is a *recit—in tempo*. 'Thekla' has alternating passages of *recit* and *tempo*. Several other songs follow similarly although the phrase becomes *im Takte*. In 'Die Bürgschaft' a six bar passage is marked *recit*, two bars later *im Takt*, and two bars after that *ohne Takt*. In other songs are found such directions as *quasi recit in tempo, beinahe recit, deklamirt, taktlos*, and *ad lib.*

The very profusion of such directions makes it difficult to decide on the rendering of a passage marked merely *recit.* The above examples are from the longer works, for in the shorter ones with which we are here chiefly concerned there is rarely any qualifying remark. The first of these is 'Verklärung' in which the opening is *quasi recit* although not so expressed, and in the middle of the song there is a passage marked *recit.* Both passages should be sung as integral parts of the song, and there was no need for the second to be so marked.

It would therefore appear to be Schubert's general practice in such songs to mark in this way passages that break away from the even tenor of the rest of the work, and have neither the lyrical melody nor running accompaniment of what precedes or follows such sections. Even the last phrase of 'Erlkönig' is marked *recit*, and although Loewe ends his setting in a similar way he has not marked it so. Perhaps Schubert was over-meticulous in this matter in some cases.

The first dozen songs are a mixed lot but half of them are by Schiller to whom Schubert was much attracted, for he also set seventeen trios for men's voices to various verses by this poet, thus making a total of twenty-three Schiller settings in the seventy-seven various compositions up to the end of 1813. It is unfortunate that Schiller has not a lyrical manner really suitable for the song so that these early works are unsatisfactory, but

Schubert profited enormously by tackling them in so bold a manner, and the settings show that he was not content with writing a merely pleasant melody but wished to bring out the varied emotions of each phrase. His perseverence thus enabled him at a later date to produce the *durchkomponiert* or on-running song in perfect form.

This doggedness is apparent when we find that barely a dozen of the first fifty songs are in strophic form. 'Klaglied' is quoted as the first of these but examination of the stanzas would seem to prove that Schubert set only the first, for some of the others fit so badly that we cannot believe he would have left them thus. Although he had set one poem by Matthisson in 1813 it was in the following year that he concentrated on this poet who provided over half the songs for 1814. Here he had much easier material to hand. The tender sentiments of love and melancholy meditation brought forth melodious strains in easy four-bar sentences and generally seemed to call for a strophic setting. That only two of them were in this form was due to the uneven phrasing in some of the stanzas. With Kosegarten, who supplied twenty-one poems in 1815, the lines are complete in themselves, or in couplets, and were all set strophically, and this is also the case with the Hölty poems of 1816, but Matthisson would often (especially in the middle stanzas of a poem) run one line into the first half of the next, so that although the metre and rhyme were regular, the phrasing was not.

Hence the musical setting appropriate for some of the stanzas was unsuitable for others and Schubert found it necessary to break away from his strophic form at such points. 'Die Betende' does not need such treatment, but there are one or two slight adjustments for the sake of accent. In 'Der Geistertanz' (No. 27) the middle section is altered for effect and not for reasons of metre. 'Erinnerungen' opens:

> *Am Seegestad', in lauen Vollmondsnächten,*
> *Denk' ich nur dich!*[1]

Schubert has set this and the two following stanzas in 3 + 2 bar phrases, but stanza four opens with:

> *Am Hüttchen dort bekränzt' ich dir, umflossen*
> *Von Abendgluth,*[2]

Here the phrasing is different. It will not fit into the music of the previous stanzas and is set in recitative; the last stanza being like the first. 'Der Abend' also has a recitative section for the same reason. It is for the fourth stanza in which the time changes to four-four. The last line of this returns to the previous six-eight time and thus leads gently into the opening melody again. 'Lied aus der Ferne' presents a slightly different problem. The stanzas consist of six lines, but whereas the first and fourth stanzas are in a 4 + 2 form, the second and third have a grammatical structure of 5 + 1. Thus Schubert's musical form of 8 + 4 bars, in two bar phrases, so apt for the beginning and end, is not suitable for the middle of the song. The first four phrases are therefore extended by repeating the third, and the fifth is used for the last

---

[1] *Beside the sea, as the moonbeams shimmer,*
  I think of thee!
[2] *By the cottage I crowned thee, encompassed*
  By sunset-glow.

line. Then in order to complete the form the last line is repeated on the sixth phrase.

As the other early works are on similar lines the first twenty-four songs fall roughly into six groups.

  I Long works consisting of several sections.

  II Lyrical poems set in *durchkomponiert* style.

  III Strophic songs.

  IV Strophic songs, but with a recitative forming a middle section.

  V Short songs wholly in recitative.

  VI Songs with alternate *recit* and *cantabile* passages.

List of Songs

No.	Title	Poet	Group
1	Hagars Klage	Schücking	I
2	Des Mädchens Klage	Schiller	II
3	Eine Leichenphantasie	Schiller	I
4	Der Vatermörder	Pfeffel	I
5	Klaglied	Rochlitz	III
6	Der Jüngling am Bache	Schiller	II
7	Todtengräberlied	Hölty	II
8	Die Schatten	Matthisson	II
9	Sehnsucht	Schiller	II
10	Verklärung	Herder (Pope)	VI
11	Thekla	Schiller	VI
12	Der Taucher	Schiller	I
13	Don Gayseros	Fouqué	II

At the outset Schubert therefore covered the whole range of song-form and fixed his framework for many a magnificent work. For some unfathomable reason the later songs that fall into group I are still utterly neglected by singers. If the statement that 'after a certain time the listener loses interest in any piece of music that consists simply of voice and pianoforte'[1] is a fact, it is hard to explain. The voice is, or ought to be, more engaging than the violin, but works for this instrument with piano are listened to with interest for much longer periods than any Schubert song demands.

It is a great pity that the song form which Schubert developed from the early rambling style to such great heights in 'Viola', 'Vergissmeinnicht', 'Uraniens Flucht', 'Elysium', 'Einsamkeit' and 'Im Walde' should be condemned to oblivion. It is understandable with some of

[1] Capell, p. 178.

the ballads, a form in which Loewe is generally superior, or with 'Schiffers Scheidelied' which sadly lacks variety, but many other long songs are, if anything, too varied. This may be the case even with 'Die Erwartung' a poem which might be considered of a more popular nature and general interest than some of the others. It is also one often referred to as being based on a setting by Zumsteeg, partly in the belief that it is an early work of 1815. As however it was written in May 1816 (and even revised later)[1] it is difficult to believe that Schubert would have to refer to a minor composer. There are some resemblances in form but this is due to the poem with its alternate short and long stanzas, in the same way that Loewe's and Schubert's 'Erlkönig' have resemblances.

It was the fourth group that was the most unsatisfactory at the outset. It has been noted that the recitative section was inserted to agree with a variation in the verbal phrasing, and in one instance to form contrast. That Schubert did not like this method is proved by the fact that he eliminated it as soon as his technique had sufficiently developed. The first difficulty he overcame either by more careful selection of verse or by writing a more flexible vocal line that could be altered in phrasing according to that of the words. In 'Nachtgesang' (No. 32) the first two lines are:

> *O gieb vom weichen Pfühle,*
> *Träumend, ein halb Gehör!*[2]

[1] Maurice Brown in *Music and Letters*, October 1957, p. 363.

[2] *O give from that soft pillow,*
Dreaming, a listening ear!

The next stanza runs on for three lines without a comma, and the third runs:

> *Die ewigen Gefühle*
> *Heben mich, hoch und hehr,*[1]

The melody carries all these varieties of phrasing to perfection and it was thus that many songs which might have been in group IV are in fact splendid strophic songs in which the melody—seemingly so simple—is in fact of such pliant material that it will carry various forms of syntax.

Yet the method of contrast was not lost sight of. It could be achieved by giving alternate stanzas a different melody as in 'Trost in Thränen' (No. 33). In this it is very suitable as the odd stanzas are questions or invitations while the even ones are the answers, the first being in the major and the latter in the tonic minor. These answers are emphasized also by a repetition of the last two lines and then the last line again.

'Das Mädchen aus der Fremde' (No. 30) is more varied:

Stanza i then ½ bar rest.	Stanza ii no rest.
Stanza iii as i.	Stanza iv varied. One bar ritornello.
Stanza v as i.	Stanza vi a charming variant of ii with some of the phrases reversed, one bar coda.

The song is practically continuous, and in neither of the above is there a real contrast as each song gives an

---

[1] *These everlasting feelings*
Raise me, high and far,

impression of having only half the number of stanzas really present. It is however a form sometimes used to avoid monotony where the stanzas are short and numerous.

But Schubert still clung to his idea of a contrasting middle section, partly perhaps because he liked the ternary form, but for the more important reason that in many poems there is a change of mood or statement about half way through. In 'Abendlied der Fürstin' the peaceful scene is disturbed by the storm, in 'Schäfers Klagelied' by 'Regen, Sturm, und Gewitter', and in both cases the melodic flow is broken, in the one by a passage marked *recit,* and in the other by a contrasting section which is melodic enough not to warrant the description. The phrase 'Es schwindelt mir—' in 'Sehnsucht' is a passionate interlude in all the settings but only in the first is it marked *recit.* This song is in F but closes in A flat minor before the *recit* which works its way to C major. There is then a brief interlude to establish the original key.

The two next settings are in the minor. The one in A minor passes straight into the sub-dominant for 'Es schwindelt—' and closes on the dominant for the reprise. The other is similarly related and it is interesting to note that in all three the cadence at the end of the passage is introduced by an augmented sixth. There are two further settings (Op. 62) and in all except the first the passage under discussion is closely related at its opening and close to the original key although all contain rather tempestuous harmonies.

Such points seem to prove that Schubert marked those

sections as *recit* which are in some way or other rather
alien to the main body of the work, but as soon as he
was able to deviate strongly while yet maintaining the
threads of unity there was no reason for noting the fact.
Even in one of his last songs, 'Am Meer', there is a passage very similar to the one noted above, but the listener,
although keenly aware of the alteration of scene and
emotion, does not perceive that it is in fact a recitative
passage. To such fine art had the composer brought his
first efforts that examination will show many dozens of
songs in which the music has a ternary form of *cantabile
—declamatory—cantabile*. Some, like 'Der Sieg' and 'Der
Lindenbaum' are fairly obvious, but in many others,
such as 'Einsamkeit', 'Die Krähe' and 'Die Nebensonnen'
the change is much more subtle.

Group VI merges into group I. It is a relic of the *recit*
and *aria*, and as such may be observed in 'Die abgeblühte
Linde', 'Die Allmacht', etc. In such songs recitative passages are apposite but they were used less and less as
composition progressed, as may be noted by the fact
that the number of songs containing marked recitative
diminished each year. They are:

28 in Nos.   1—100
11 in Nos. 101—200
14 in Nos. 201—414

The long works of later years are found in group II and
stanza follows stanza with ever new melody or with
similar melody in which various slight alterations enable
it to follow the changing mood of the words. A large
number of these have a figured accompaniment of the

kind that is first found to perfection in 'Gretchen am Spinnrade'. However much the melody fluctuates in rhythm and outline such a piano part forms a wonderful means of unity and Schubert could produce the most significant 'themes' for such accompaniments—the wild surge of storm music whether of the elements or the heart, the rippling brook and the calm or violent sea, or even the twinkling stars and the heart-throbs of the lover. The other two groups (III and V) also merge. The strophic song took on a wide variety of character from the simple melody of 'Das Wandern' to the complexity of 'Das Irrlicht', or became completely recitative as in 'Der Leiermann'. This range is truly marvellous. In the most simple there is always some point of interest, and a very large number are masterpieces of germinal music in which lies hidden the expression of quite diverse stanzas. Despite the glory of the great *durchkomponiert* songs, it is perhaps in the strophic form of a large part of the song-cycles that Schubert shows his greatest genius.

His gift of significant melody has already been mentioned. His predecessors in song composition produced many charming works but in few cases do their settings seem inevitable. The melody is generally suitable but no more, and the accompaniments are thin and have nothing to add to the vocal line. Reichardt's 'Jägers Abendlied' consists of two four-bar phrases. The melody is a simple hunting-horn tune with an accompaniment of plain chords which are nearly all on the tonic. Its connection with the words is negligible except for the preliminary sign *pp*. Schubert on the other hand notes the opening 'Im Felde schleich' ich' and writes an accompaniment of sliding sixths. The second half of the stanza becomes sentimental and the music becomes more emotional with passing chromatic chords.

Reichardt's setting of 'Hoffnung' has an attractive lilt,

Ex. 2. Die Hoffnung   *Reichardt(1810)*

and in the opening words 'There speak and dream many men of better days—of a happy golden time' he stresses the second word. Schubert produced a simple version of the song in 1815 and in 1819 a better one with the Reichardt rhythm, but his melody does not rise until the second syllable of 'traümen', and then only by a fifth. The leap of a major sixth is reserved for 'glücklichen' (happy) in the third line, thereby suggesting that dreamers of happiness are more important than mere talkers.

Zelter's 'Der Musensohn' is in two-bar phrases, $a+a+b+c+c+d$, with a slight accompaniment nearly all

on the tonic and a half-close at *b*. Schubert's setting
is too famous to need quotation. Schulz's version of
'Abendlied' (Der Mond ist aufgegangen) consists of a six-
bar sentence, repeated and lengthened by two beats to
close on the tonic—a charming construction. The melody
(Example 3) is hymn-like in peace and serenity.

Ex.3. Abendlied *Schulz (1790)*

Der Mond ist auf-ge-gan - gen, die

sanft und leise

goldnen Sternlein pran-gen am Himmel hell und clar;

Opposed to this static quality Schubert's setting is
kinetic in its vision of the rising moon and the sparkling
stars. It is in 6/8 instead of 4/4 and also of twelve bars,
with a delightful little coda. The opening melody springs
up lightly from the dominant to the mediant, then up

to sub-dominant and then up to the high dominant. Schulz's setting has been most highly praised,[1] but if Schubert missed the mark in the opening stanzas he has caught the whimsical turn of the poet when he suggests that although the moon is full and round only half of it is visible, and this may be so with many things, including ourselves.

[1] Einstein, pp. 26 and 161.

II

PHRASING AND FORM

S C H U B E R T ' S success in song is evidence of a very
original mind, even though this was linked with a certain
diffidence which caused him to follow too closely the
recognized forms in instrumental music. It was some
years before he could break through this formal con-
straint, but in the realm of song there were no great and
awe-inspiring works to set a standard and defy com-
petition to youth. Here there was scope for originality
in form in its broadest sense. In a very limited sense we
may say that there is no song form for it cannot follow
any general outline like those of first movement or
rondo.

Primarily the poem is the deciding factor in the for-
mation of a song. It influences length, phrasing and
variety, but within these vague limits there is much
freedom. We cannot in fact judge the length of a poem
by its setting, for by repetition, by long notes in the
melody and by various interludes a short poem may
become an extensive song; and a long poem in a strophic
setting may be a shorter composition. The phrasing
may be expanded or contracted and in general the
poem illuminated and interpreted in a very individual
manner.

It is not only in the significance of melody and accompaniment that Schubert revolutionized the song. He gave it flexibility and variety of form. Even the simple two and four bar phrases have individuality. Reichardt set 'Heidenröslein' in 1793 and Schubert in 1815. Both are in 2/4 time and consist of seven two-bar phrases, but the latter has more varied harmony and thus more rhythmic motion, and there is a *fermata* near the end followed by a *rallentando*. Then there is a pause on the high tonic; but because of the beautifully balanced phrasing this lingering, rising scale of nearly an octave arouses a sense of expectation which is fully satisfied by the last two bars *wie oben*. This is great art and may be observed continually in an enormous number of the songs which are in two and four bar phrases. This form is as natural in music as the couplet in verse or the rectangle which encloses a drawing. It is what is in them that counts, and in music and verse it is the sequence of phrases that is so important, for it is only when the mind is carried along in expectation that there is true vitality.

This quality is inherent in the Schubertian melody, the harmony of which flows onward like the river he loved so much. In very few songs could we be misled as to the actual conclusion, for if the phrases themselves are conclusive the accompaniment or a following *ritornello* carries us onward.

A simple verse like 'Winterlied':

> *Keine Blumen blühn;*
> *Nur das Wintergrün*
> *Blickt durch Silberhüllen;*

Nur das Fenster füllen
Blumen roth und weiss,
Aufgeblüht aus Eis.[1]

could be set quite easily as a jog-trot sort of folk-song, but the fact that Schubert's setting is twelve bars in length does not imply two bars to the line. The phrasing is $2 + 1\frac{1}{2} + 2\frac{1}{2} + 3\frac{1}{2} + 2$, and then $2\frac{1}{2}$ bars coda. The second and third lines are closely connected by a kind of overlap, and the fourth and fifth are compressed in the $3\frac{1}{2}$ bars. The lengthening of a phrase by a simple harmonic progression is used in extended form in 'Auf den Tod einer Nachtigall' in which the lines consist of alternate eleven and four syllables. Even then some of the lines run in pairs so that there is no definite break in the whole of each stanza. The first stanza is phrased $2 + 4 + 8 + 2 + 6 + 8 + 3$ and the last line is repeated in two bars instead of three. But some of these phrases are indeterminate in that their cadences are deceptive and thus allow for the melody to run on where required in other stanzas, so that the whole composition is flexible and purposeful with a gentle pressure onward to the final cadence in spite of the very slow tempo.

Even in the earliest songs examples of varied phrasing are to be found. In 'Klaglied' the two first lines are in four bars but are repeated in two with the lines inverted. 'Die Betende' may be compared with the lovely setting

[1] *Not a flower is seen;*
Only evergreen
Shows through snowy mantle;
On the window-panes we
See the flowers white
Blooming in the night.

by Zelter which is in four-bar phrases the squareness of which is veiled by the melodic curve and varied accompaniment. (Example 4).

Ex.4. Die Betende   *Zelter (1794)*

Lau - ra   be - tet Engels harfen hal - len,

Schubert's phrasing is 5+4+6+3 and the harmonies are richer, while the sequence after the two first words, slightly altered to agree with the phrasing of the next stanza, lifts it right out of the folk-song form. In 'Der Abend' the lines of four feet are at first in two-bar phrases, but the last half of the stanza is expanded to phrases of two and a half bars by the lengthening of the first word of each line to a whole bar. In 'Naturgenuss' the first two lines are 4 + 3; the next two are 2 + 2; but the last line of the latter is repeated to a melody of four bars. The repetitive process is extended in 'Stimme der Liebe' as the last line is first of two bars and then repeated in two and a half bars and then again in three.

The repetition of words and phrases has caused some criticism, and in the early works there is little justification for the practice except occasionally when an important phrase is stressed—as 'ich finde' in 'Gretchen am Spinnrade'. In many later songs the effect is excellent.

In 'Die abgeblühte Linde' there is no repetition until the neglect of the tree is mentioned, and this is repeated in a beautiful sequence a tone higher. The reason for this is clear as the last couplet follows, for it embodies a sentiment well worth the elaborate expression which Schubert gives it on the final page with a beautiful cadence which emphasizes the last line at its first appearance.

> *Nur der Gartner bleibt ihr treu,*
> *Denn er liebt in ihr den Baum.*[1]

These lines are developed for about forty bars and are a splendid example of the expansive quality of music. The poet can only repeat his lines to a very limited extent, and if he elaborates a sentiment he is more than likely to introduce some fresh idea or train of thought because of the connotative power of words. But the musician may dwell much longer on the thought and thus impress us more deeply even if only by the fact that there is more time in which to apprehend it; and there seems no valid reason why he should not do so. This is a song of 1817 and if composed ten years later it might have been set in the style of the *Winterreise,* but its broad outlines and the tenderness of the lingering phrases make us prefer it as it is.

'Im Walde' (Schlegel) has many repetitions but their fascinating variety over the vast compass of the piano part gives them justification. At first they are mere ejaculations in the wind and storm but become fierce striding figures as powerful as those in the storm of the

---

[1] *Only the gardener remains true to it,*
For he loves the tree for itself.

'Pastoral' Symphony. Even the sparkling section in C has repetitions in order to give it breadth commensurate with the rest of the song.

In 'Der zürnenden Diana' the repetitions enable the song to become a mountainous outburst of emotion in which the voice soars in big phrases comparable to the *Liebestod*. Like 'Im Walde' it is, as regards form, one of Schubert's biggest songs; for in spite of the look of the printed page there are few modulations, and the whole work is unified by the use of either the treble or bass of the opening bar. In the C major section the appoggiatura figure in the treble is derived from the treble of the first part and then when the treble takes over the *tremolo* the bass carries on with that of the first part. (See also p. 62). It is thus in a kind of ternary form in the keys of A flat —C—A flat. In the first part the key is maintained for thirty-four bars before a true modulation occurs. This seems to be C flat (B major) but then the harmony hovers between D flat, G flat and C flat until it closes on E flat, which is immediately sharpened for a short interlude in E major. Then follows the middle section which continues in C major for thirty-five bars, and then the last section in A flat again for sixty-four bars.

The expansion of phrases adds musical delight and significance to many a song. The lines of 'Danksagung an den Bach' are generally one bar in length so that with the anacrusis they end on the third beat (of four quavers). But instead of crowding 'war es' at the end of the bar after 'Klingen' a beat rest is inserted so that these words now come on the second beat and the phrase ends on a strong beat. Then, after the next two lines, 'gelt' does not immediately follow after 'Sinn' but is given a whole bar to itself. Yet in spite of these and other variants in vocal phrasing the song swings smoothly and gently along over the flowing accompaniment in perfect measure. Another interesting point here is that the poet has italicized the 'sie' in the third stanza—'Hat *sie* dich geschickt'[1] and 'Ob *sie*' but Schubert has not marked them in any way. They are of normal length on the first beat but they stand out because on the first the harmony changes suddenly to the tonic minor (of G) and on the second there is a dominant seventh on F natural.

In 'Muth' all the phrases are of two bars except the first and third. Here the words 'Schnee' and 'Herz' are lengthened, thus forming three bar phrases and not only emphasizing those words but accentuating the cynical agitation of the following lines.

The miller in 'Am Feierabend', after wishing for untold strength which would make him outstanding among his fellows, says that the miller is pleased with all their work. This is satisfactory and worth repeating, but when the maiden wishes them all good night the desire to be especially favoured makes him repeat this phrase after a *sf* chord which strongly emphasizes 'all' in a melancholy manner, the main point of the song being that at present he is merely one of many in her eyes instead of being 'all' to her.

A beautiful example of the closing-in of phrases occurs between the second and third lines of 'Litanei' which are run into three bars instead of the expected four; so that there are $1\frac{3}{4} + 1\frac{1}{4}$ instead of $2 + 2$. In 'An die

[1] Has *she* sent you.

Leyer' the last stanza on repetition is shortened by one
bar. At first 'So lebt denn wohl' follows a *ritornello* of
one and three quarter bars but in the repeat the voice
enters above this and the following word 'Heroen' is
a bar further back in the accompaniment than it was
before, and a whole bar of the piano part is therefore
cut out. The first vocal sentence in 'Pilgerweise' is a sad
melody of eight bars, the next blossoms out richly in
the major but is only seven bars long.

Repetitions themselves provide many points of interest.
In 'Im Frühling' the cadences fall in the middle of the
bar and the last line, 'I was so happy', closes in A minor,
but is then quickly repeated in G major to end on a
strong beat. Hence a change from the sadness of recollec-
tion to the happiness of the memory is attained by a
mere repetition of three words. Schubert, who at first
had difficulty in maintaining his form at a sudden
emotional change in the poem could later insert such
changes as were hidden in the words, or even beyond the
verbal expression of many of the minor poets he selected.

The last line of each stanza in 'An mein Herz' is
repeated. If the second stanza followed the pattern of
the first it would run 'so/ mag's verloren/ sein',[1] but it
is phrased—'so/ mag's verloren, ver/loren/ sein, so mag's
ver/loren/ sein'. Thus although there is an extension of
the line there is also anticipation and a sense of syncopa-
tion to give a feeling of emotional stress as the first
syllable of 'verloren' is hurried in order to lengthen the
second one.

[1] *I might have lost it then* (verloren=lost, and is untranslatable
in three syllables).

There is a powerful contrast of phrasing in 'Die Wetterfahne'. The line 'Der Wind spielt drinnen—', like the opening line, occupies two bars. The question 'Was fragen sie nach meinem Schmerz?' is compressed into a bar and a half. The former is marked *leise* and the latter *laut*; one of the few cases in which Schubert gives specific directions to the singer. So in 'Rückblick', the major section is in two bar phrases, but in the agitated opening most of the phrases are paired together in three bars. Then in 'Rast' the line 'Die Füsse frugen nicht nach Rast' is half a bar shorter than the other phrases. In the next stanza the line is normal (Auch du, mein Herz,).

There is a similar speed-up of the unimportant syllables of 'Ich bin so glücklich, bin so reich' in 'Der blinde Knabe' in order to bring the fourth and seventh words on a strong accent. The whole of this song is worth study for the phrasing alone. It is a beautiful work and no doubt Capell would have written more highly of it had he not been offended by the subject of the poem, to which he does an injustice by quoting only the first and last stanzas. It is the other three that give some justification to the sentiment. Palgrave thought highly enough of it to include it in his *Golden Treasury*. Capell says the accompaniment is 'one of the prettiest of its kind in Schubert'—it suggested 'a graceful and placid brook song'. But the brook music is in closer harmony than these wide-spread arpeggios, and the manner in which the bass figure sinks to momentary rest on the two quavers has some similarity in form and expression with the treble of 'Auflösung' which also swirls in arpeggio and then comes to an almost stationary shimmer. There are many songs about sunshine and moonlight but only these in which light itself is depicted.

That fine address to the sun, 'An die Sonne',[1] also illustrates a condensed phrasing. The first four bars each have four syllables but the next has six in order to give prominence to the last word of 'Hoch gegrüsst in deiner Pracht!' The next lines revert to the previous metre and the word 'das' is therefore on the first beat of a bar:

> *Golden fliesst schon/um die Hügel/*
> *Dein Gewand, und/das Geflügel/—*[2]

But the stress is negatived by the melodic form and tone, for the word 'um' is on an A natural from which the voice mounts upwards in conjunct motion to a high A flat on the middle syllable of 'Geflügel', and there is a *crescendo* from *pp* which culminates on *f* on that syllable.

Schubert has often been accused of false accentuation, but there is much to be said in his defence.[3] In fact Umlauff's account of the argument on the 'Wanderer' shows that Schubert considered such matters seriously. Umlauff insisted that the last word of 'O Land, wo bist du' should be stressed, but Schubert stuck to his opinion that 'bist' should have the emphasis. A criticism of the setting of the line 'Ich bin noch jung' with the accent on the second word has been made[4] but in this and other similar cases it is the normal manner of speech, as the orator emphasizes an 'and' when he is going to add an important clause, and just as Schubert does in 'Pilgerweise' at the

---

[1] By C. A. Tiedge: previously Anon. (see D. no. 272).
[2] *Golden flows now o'er the hill-tops*
  Thy bright robe, and all the wildfowl—
[3] See Capell, pp. 44-47.
[4] Schubert, A symposium, p. 158.

phrase 'könnt ihr dies arme Herz erquicken und es befrein'[1] which on repetition has a long tied note for 'und' with an *fp* mark. He was not infallible but he generally had good reason for what he did.

Schubert's phrases always flow easily, but with such internal stresses and strains within each song it is remarkable how a feeling of continuity is preserved after the first struggles with recitative had brought success. The points in each sentence are made and clearly perceived by the listener but it is only the critical ear or observation of the music that enables one to see the means by which they are carried out. What looks like the rather spasmodic recitative of 'Dass sie hier gewesen' is found to be almost wholly in four-bar phrases. On the other hand the very regular structure of 'Fischerweise' is broken in the last stanza to emphasize the 'schlauer Wicht' although the listener is aware only of the outstanding phrase and not the deviation in form. So in 'Der Leiermann' there is a variant in the last stanza, especially at the line 'soll ich mit dir gehn?' which is delayed by a rest so that it is the only phrase to end on a strong beat.

A glance at the last page of 'Aufenthalt' gives one an impression that the climax has passed when the reprise commences, but the thirteenth bar of this takes the top F again and then bursts out on the top G (*fff*) for the culminating climax. Freedom of form, intensity of purpose, and power of expression with the most simple means reach the highest peak of perfection in these last songs. In 'Der Doppelgänger' the piano has four-bar phrases, while the voice proceeds in twos with each

---

[1] *You may this sad heart enliven* and *free it.*

phrase commencing on the dominant until the line 'Da steht auch ein Mensch'. This starts on the mediant so that the voice has a bigger range up to the first big climax in which the phrase is lengthened. This building up process occurs twice more and the vocal line is so free that its melodious contours are apt to be overlooked. All is derived from the opening phrases except the condensed line 'das mich gequält—' which has the passionate rising phrase so characteristically Schubertian (e.g. 'Der Atlas'), and the final long-drawn-out line somewhat like that of 'In der Ferne'. There is also the harmonic passage rising in semitones at the *accelerando* which is also a characteristic response to mounting agony such as the similar but extended phrases of 'Fragen sich einander' in 'Gruppe aus Tartarus'. So much depends on the harmony in these songs that further study is deferred to a later chapter.

III

KEY

SCHUBERT'S sense of note relationship whether in melody or harmony was extraordinarily keen, and of all notes he held the mediant as the most expressive. It was of course the means of major-minor transformation which is such a characteristic of his work, but it was much more than this. His melodies so often revolve around that note, rising to it in conjunct or disjunct motion, using it as a climax or as an initial opening of a fresh phrase, or making it a pivot for modulation. In all the greater songs the third of almost every chord seems to be 'placed' with loving care, and regardless of the ordinary diatonic scale it is turned into a major or minor interval according to his feeling for the word or phrase in the song.

This is the reason for his chromatic harmonies and modulations. We know that on the notes of the major scale three of the triads are major and three are minor, but Schubert had no hesitation in altering this state of affairs whenever he thought it necessary. Sevenths are frequent so that they may fall to a third and thus receive prominence, and other discords sometimes receive an unusual resolution for the same purpose. The half close in a minor key is a favourite cadence because of the final major third which adds pathos to the phrase in many an instance, as for example in the beautiful lines of 'Leiden der Trennung'. (Example 5).

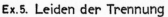

Ex.5. Leiden der Trennung

In 'Mit dem grünen Lautenbande' the second phrase rises to D from B flat as though to modulate to the relative minor but, as the melody continues in B flat, the D major chord should be considered a major triad on the mediant.

Although the songs show in their many and varied modulations the keenest perception of key relationship Schubert does not seem to have a partiality for a key *per se*.[1] He was not generally averse to transposition and probably only avoided extreme keys for the benefit of the performer, and we know that publishers demanded this of him at times. In fact the initial key of a song is of little importance, for the deviations from it by chromatic chords and modulation often lead into distant spheres from which there is no return; a quite natural process when the verses have travelled far from the sentiment of the opening lines and the aesthetic requirements of absolute music are no longer applicable. Schubert should therefore be commended for *not* always concluding a song in the opening key, for any attempt to do this would have sacrificed the emotional development in such cases to a mere formality. In the very long songs the opening key is soon lost to memory; hence there is no need to return

[1] See, however, *Schubert* by M. J. E. Brown where there are several references to a relationship between key and mood.

to it unless the lines recapitulate the opening in some way (as in 'Viola'), but in the shorter songs which close in a 'foreign' key it would appear that Schubert had in mind the climax of the song and set his key for this, using the first part to lead up to it.

Hence there is often not much guidance in stating the key of a song except perhaps for identification, and in a good many cases it is impossible to do so. 'Orest auf Tauris' (1820) has a signature of three flats. The first chords are C minor, a seventh on B flat, and then E flat, followed by a short phrase in B flat. (Example 6).

Ex.6. Orest auf Tauris.

The whole is repeated a fourth higher to close on E flat, leading to E flat minor and its relative major for seventeen bars. Then the key changes to B major for two lines, while the last page is in D major. The latter is therefore the ruling key and is related to the opening chords by being a tone higher than C minor or a semitone lower than E flat, and as both these relationships are often used by Schubert we are still no wiser as to the opening key.

This ambiguity occurs even in the early songs. 'Die Mondnacht' (1815) is in F sharp major according to the key signature and final cadence but the four-bar prelude is in B major. 'Nähe des Geliebten' (1815) is in G flat but the prelude opens on the chord of B flat major and works its way in two bars to an augmented sixth on the subdominant. As the voice enters this sixth resolves on the first inversion of the tonic so that although the key is established by the voice there is no full close until the end of the second line:

> *Ich denke dein, wenn mir der Sonne Schimmer*
> *Vom Meere strahlt;*[1]

This beautiful harmonic phrasing arouses the interest of the listener leading him onward to the verbal cadence, and here we find one vital reason for the delay in 'key fixation'. In 'Grenzen der Menschheit' the key signature (E) refers chiefly to the tender second stanza. The prelude is mainly in C and it is not until bar twenty that there is a full close in E; but even then chromatic harmonies veil the key until the entrance of 'küss ich—'. 'Freiwilliges Versinken' is a similar case in one flat. In the four opening bars there are two chords of A major but they do not proceed to D minor, and in bars 6-7 there is a cadence to F major which gradually modulates (in bar 16) to D minor and the last page of the song fluctuates between that key and its tonic major. Many other examples of this deliberate restraint from establishing the key could be quoted. 'Dass sie hier gewesen' consists largely of the diminished seventh on C sharp until the words of the title occur in the most simple of C major phrases, which is obviously the 'burden' of the song.

Sometimes a minor seventh on the tonic is used to veil the key, as in 'Am Fenster' where the third chord, in the

---

[1] *I think of thee, whene'er the sun-rays' shimmer*
  The sea reflects;

key of F, has an E flat. The phrase is however so delicately constructed that it still retains the sense of F major. The phrase is repeated twice before the song modulates to F minor in which key the flattened leading note still persists. A beautiful example (from 1815) of this process is found in 'An die Geliebte', in G major. The first chord is C, the next a minor seventh on G going to A minor. In bar seven there is a passing cadence in G (that is to say the dominant—tonic progression occurs in the middle of a phrase) so that in fact we do not come to a conclusive full close in G until the end of the song, twenty-four bars from the opening. Schubert used the first phrase of this song a year later in 'An die Nachtigall' (Claudius) but made it into an eight-bar sentence closing in the tonic.

Before leaving the subject of key signatures a numerical list may be of interest if the above notes are borne in mind.

Key	major	minor	
C	44		36
G	46		31
D	23		34
A	49		34
E	36		18
B	11		19
F sharp	—		5
F	49		17
B flat	45		5
E flat	35		3
A flat	38		1
D flat	7	C sharp	3
G flat	7	G sharp	1
	390		207

Not much can be deduced from these facts. There is a slight preponderance of flat over sharp keys. The small number of minor songs in the flat keys may be explained by the large number of accidentals involved especially when there is much modulation. Of the songs in C major only about half a dozen are among the great works, but of those in C minor there are over a dozen. It is interesting to note that in three of the most powerful songs the climax is in C major. 'Heliopolis' II (Fels auf Felsen) opens in C minor, but the last page breaks magnificently into the major with a fine descending bass. The triumphant finale of 'Prometheus' (in B flat) is also in C major, as is that of 'Gruppe aus dem Tartarus'. The latter song has a key signature of C major or minor—but neither key emerges until the outburst at 'Ewigkeit' in the major which is prepared by four bars of C minor (at bar 60!). The song in the awkward key of A flat minor is 'Auf dem Wasser zu singen' but this is another case of retarded key. The song is really in the major and the first part is 'minored' with accidentals until the beautiful modulation occurs. That in G sharp minor is 'Du liebst mich nicht', but was published in 1826 in A minor.

Major and minor

Schubert's major-minor alteration is so famous that many examples are well known. Even in instrumental works he preferred fluctuating colour and emotion to the magnificent tonal architecture of Beethoven, and in the songs it is of fundamental importance. The poet delights in contrast and Schubert followed most willingly whether in stanzas, phrases or even single words. A very beautiful instance of the first case occurs in 'Pilgerweise' where the first stanza in F sharp minor is followed by the second in the tonic major; of the second case in Hölty's 'An den Mond' as the first line changes from F minor to its relative major. Another instance is in 'Aus Heliopolis' I. Here the first stanza and two lines of the second are in E minor. The key signature then changes to E major, but here again we have a delayed action for the next three lines really vacillate between A and B major, and the flower's reply 'Wende, so wie ich' enters quite clearly in the key of E.

In 'Erlafsee', as 'so wohl, so weh' is repeated a minor ninth occurs on the second 'so', and as the sun 'flimmert blässer' the chord changes from F major to minor. In 'Wehmuth' (Collin) the words 'wohl und weh' also occur but as the first two words are on a major dominant chord it merely changes to the minor on the third word. The repetition of 'entschwindet' is on a first inversion of the D major chord but it is echoed on the piano with the bottom note lowered a semitone to F natural. 'Schwestergrüss', in F sharp minor, closes on the three last significant words in the tonic major. This song also illustrates the delay in fixing the key, for the first two bars contain only reiterated C sharps. Then the third below is added, and the harmony develops to prove that the first notes presage a long dominant upper pedal in the minor.

This intentional vagueness is of great emotional significance. The first bar of 'Erlkönig' with its bare octaves sets the scene and stirs the mind: and although enjoyment of the song grows with acquaintance it is at a first hearing that such an initial phrase rouses most interest, for the mind of the listener, even unconsciously, must be attempting to fix a tonality. Such a phrase as opens 'Der Schmetterling' attracts our attention. It is in the key of F whereas we should expect C. 'An Rosa' I is clearer because of the first two notes, and in the opening of 'Die Götter Griechenlands' we imagine the dominant chord on the semiquaver although there is nothing but bare sixths and fifths until the fourth bar. Such devices have a subtle effect in the mind. Bare fourths and fifths echo down the ages and set up sympathetic vibrations in the mind, the profundity and significance of which is not realized by the intellect. Great composers know this instinctively and there is no more marvellous example than the long passage of fifths that forms the opening of the 'Choral' Symphony.[1] It is such processes that Schubert also handles with such skill and he can be as deeply impressive with the minimum of expressions as in the biggest and most involved harmonic passages.

The major third

Some writers have exaggerated the minor aspect of Schubert's music, whereas it is on the major third that he concentrated much more.[2] His melodies dwelt lovingly on that note wherever possible and his harmonies flowed in a way that gave it prominence. For example there are sixty-one notes for the voice in 'An die Musik' and of these nineteen are on the third of a major chord. In the

[1] See Shaw's *Music in London*, p. 154, for a remarkable observation on a bare fifth in *Les Huguenots*.

[2] See E Blom, *Music and Letters*, October; 1928, 'His favourite device'.

G major section of 'Der Musensohn' the proportion is twenty-nine to sixty-one. All the happiest songs commence on the major mediant, or approach it on the strong beat. The approximate numbers are:

(a) Commencing on the mediant   76
(b) Commencing on leap from dominant up to mediant 20
(c) Prominent mediant on 2nd or 3rd note   36
         (excluding b)

The songs in which the mediant, although present, is not significant have been excluded from these figures, which give the rather staggering total of 132 or nearly a quarter of the songs. This does not imply that they are all happy songs for the mood may change once or more times, but the same thing happens in the minor songs in many of which a change is heralded by an immediate prominence of the major third.

The songs with an anacrusis in which the voice leaps from the dominant to the mediant have been listed separately (b) because this leap of a major sixth is characteristic of a happy serenity such as that found in 'Der Einsame', the opening of Mayrhofer's 'Der Sieg' and 'Sehnsucht', 'Das Fischermädchen', and in four of the *Müllerlieder*. The latter are nos. 3, 7, 8 and 12, while nos. 2, 4, 10, 11, 13, and the second part of 19 and 20 all begin on the mediant although in some this note is on a weak beat.

Numbers 5 and 15 commence with the leap of a minor sixth and belong to a small group in which the pathos is expressed thus at the outset. The minor third itself is not stressed to the same extent as the major. Although sixteen songs in the *Winterreise* are in the minor only two of

D

them commence on the mediant. Several of them open with a phrase on the notes of the tonic chord or on the dominant itself. The first note of 'Gute Nacht' is an interesting case for although it is on the up beat its position as the highest note of the phrase gives it additional emphasis and brings forward the word 'Fremd'[1] which is practically a key-word for the whole cycle. It is on the minor mediant and when the last stanza opens in the tonic major this note becames transformed in the most tender manner. Its use in the last line is another touch of genius. 'An dich hab' ich gedacht' says the 'Fremde' lovingly, and then repeats the phrase in the minor as though realizing that he has doomed himself by 'thinking of her'.

In both 'Auf dem Flusse' and 'Rückblick' the thought of happy days (in the second stanza) is ushered in with the major mediant, both in the tonic major. In 'Der Lindenbaum' and 'Die Post' the opposite process takes place. Of the major songs in this cycle five give prominence to the mediant in the first bar, 'Frühlingstraum' commencing with the major sixth leap. The slow pace and full chords of 'Das Wirthshaus' give it solemnity while the introduction of the B flat in the first phrase adds a touch of sadness, and here again the last stanza takes up the phrase in the tonic minor; but at the mention of 'mein treuer Wanderstab' the major again appears—his trusty staff is all that is left to him. 'Die Nebensonnen' is similar in these respects. The subdominant note is again inserted between the mediants (in 'am Himmel steh'n')

[1] 'Stranger'—somewhat in our sense of 'foreigner' in a village community.

and this, with the dying fall of the other mediants, gives the whole sentence a pathos that belies its major mode.

There is another method by which the mediant is emphasized. This is based on the notes of the dominant seventh between an upper and lower mediant. Its chief purpose is to lead to that lower note which is sometimes delayed by an appoggiatura. It is familiar in 'An die Musik', commencing on the third syllable of 'zu warmer Lieb, entzunden'. The same phrase is found in:

'Der gute Hirte' at 'im kühlen Thaue'.
'Wanderers Nachtlied' at 'ach, ich bin des Treibens müde'
'Todesmusik' at 'noch einmal die stillen Lieder' and the following line (without upper mediant)
'Die Knabenzeit'—bars 8-12 (without appoggiatura)

There are many varieties of this phrase in some of which it is continued beyond the mediant. In 'Dem Unendlichen' the phrase springs up to the supertonic and then descends as usual but a turn on the lower mediant brings a conclusion on the tonic at the end of 'kein Jubel genug besingt!'. In 'Der Einsame' is a similar phrase at 'bleibt man noch gern am Feuerwach' except that the final turn concludes on the mediant.

A good many passages cannot be said to have a key for the harmony is in a continual state of flux, and no sooner has one modulatory passage arrived at a cadence than it is followed by another. In Mayrhofer's 'Einsamkeit' the first section opens and closes in B flat, but after a couple of lines the harmonies become chromatic, touch on the keys of D flat, A flat and G flat which becomes

enharmonically F sharp, then F sharp minor, D, C minor
and so on without settlement until the close. The following *geschwind* opens in F sharp but then goes on in a
long series of kaleidoscopic changes to conclude on the
dominant seventh of E. The whole of these three pages
retains the key signature of B flat and illustrates one
enigma in Schubert's scoring, for we often fail to see
why he does, or does not, change that signature at a
certain point. Later in this song there is a 'Frisch' section
of two bars only for which the key is altered from D to
C and then to F, and still later a B minor section changes
to C for over a page in which there is only one single
chord of C major, and one of C minor, after which the
key changes to G.

In 'Elysium' between the A major and D flat major
sections there is a passage of six bars with the key signature of C, which carries out the modulation that could
have been written without change of signature, and after
eleven bars the D flat key alters again to C. This latter
section is almost wholly in the key of F sharp major and
then modulates to D, under which key signature the
whole of the previous three sections (C—D flat—C) is
repeated. Perhaps it is the sort of writing that frightens
singers from this and several other beautiful songs. It
does look rather chaotic but the final result is far otherwise, and more than repays the initial study and analysis
required. In the following *lebhaft* the intention is clearer.
Here again the signature is C, but after the majestic
opening phrase the rest of the page is in E flat. Halfway
through there is a cadence to the chord of G major which
is followed immediately by E flat again. But when the

whole of this is repeated that chord becomes the dominant of C so that the last half then agrees with the key signature.

It is thus vital to examine the key structure in studying the songs, not in an abstract manner, but in order to observe their purpose, for each change is an indication of Schubert's interpretation of the emotion underlying the poet's expression.

IV

HARMONY

ALTHOUGH we have no record of Schubert's precocity as an infant his brother Ferdinand wrote that at eleven years old he had 'already composed some small songs, string quartets and pianoforte pieces', and that 'his compositions (such as Hagar's Lament, etc.) induced Salieri to give him lessons in composition'.[1] His sensitivity not only to melodic outline but to the blending of various notes must have enabled him to compose almost by instinct, and he had only to learn to write in musical notation in order to express the sounds in his mind.

A child with the genius of a Mozart or Schubert must accumulate an immense amount of aural knowledge before he is able to formulate more or less abstract harmonic theories, a later study of which serves mainly to bring into the realm of codified knowledge the material already in the mind. The sounds are known before the symbols, and musical thought is logical before formal analysis can be undertaken. The study of harmony and counterpoint may lead to perfection, but the groundwork has already been fixed in the early years and therefore this type of genius is not revolutionary in technique. Instead of inventing new means of expression its efforts are channelled into expressing a growing knowledge of life

[1] *The Documents*, p. 913.

and emotion with the technique already to hand. This technique develops because it has to carry more pregnant meaning, but it does not alter basically. It is an inward evolution and not a superimposed intellectual revolution that has to be observed in such cases.

Schubert's works abound in chromatic chords and passages and, as very often these appear at first sight to be modulatory, it is perhaps necessary to point out that he does not modulate so frequently as is sometimes suggested. Tovey deals at length with the question of 'When is a key not a key?',[1] and proves that an alien 'dominant' seventh does not form a modulation. He calls it an enhanced dominant, and argues that a key is not established until it is firmly fixed. Hence in many of the songs there are 'suggested' modulations arising from the use of chromatic chords. In 'Der Neugierige' which opens in B major the middle of the four-bar introduction has E sharps but this does not imply an entry into the key of F sharp. It establishes the original key quite firmly. The last part of 'An die Leyer' which is in E flat contains a minor seventh on the tonic, one on the submediant, and a diminished seventh on the sharpened tonic, but the melodic framework keeps the whole passage within the original key.

As this method is of such frequent occurrence an analysis of some of Schubert's favourite harmonies will illustrate more clearly the methods he used to illuminate the very wide range of his texts.

He used the classical chromatic chords freely and purposefully either for their capacity to point a phrase

[1] See *Beethoven*, p. 14.

or to colour a harmonic progression. Sometimes they stand out boldly and at others their parts so flow in the general texture of the writing that their presence is hardly noted. This counterpoint exists not only in the use of concurrent melodies between the vocal line and the bass which is such a fine feature in many songs, but in the moving parts of harmonic passages, so many of which exhibit enchanting inner melodic phrases. This is not so readily possible when plain diatonic chords are used in a small framework as by the right use of chromatic chords, and it is important to note that much of Schubert's harmony arises from his contrapuntal thought. In the early songs discords and chromatic chords are used almost as freely as in the later ones but on what may be called a 'short-term' policy. They emphasize a word or the peak of a climax, point a question or express a sigh, but as practice became more perfect these chords were antici-pated in a subtle way so that their separate notes form part of a rising or falling line. Sometimes indeed they appear with dramatic suddenness, but most often some of their notes are of great significance in a phrase, and thus the whole chord, while not obtrusive in itself, is of vital importance in the texture of the passage. Its presence has been predetermined by converging melodic lines and its parts rise or fall according to the progression of the phrase to fresh development or to a cadence. Examination of the examples quoted later will show into which categories the chords generally fall.

There are thus at least three reasons for Schubert's harmonic system, using the latter phrase to denote his treatment of chords so often used by others in different ways. There is the use of the chord *per se*, as in the opening of Heine's 'Am Meer': its use to give a phrase a strong emotional power as in 'Rastlose Liebe': and its use as a 'passing' chord to produce the smooth flowing melodic lines such as those quoted previously from 'An die Leyer'.

The Neapolitan Sixth

The triad on the flattened supertonic is known in its first inversion as the Neapolitan sixth and when used in this position is generally resolved on a dominant to form a perfect cadence. It is used in this manner for the last line of 'Der Wegweiser' (but not for the final repetition), and the introduction of 'Die Krähe'. It also concludes that tender lament 'Auf den Tod einer Nachtigall', but in the middle of this song and in the third bar of 'Die Krähe' the chord occurs in the root position. Schubert often uses this form, in which case it must be considered as one of his many chromatic chords to be used in many ways.

The sixth itself serves various purposes, a few others of which may be quoted. In 'Der Blumen Schmerz' it appears three times in the A major section to conclude minor phrases with the ordinary 'pathetic' cadence. 'Der Kampf' is in D minor and ten bars before the end there is a *fz* chord on the first inversion of the subdominant. This is followed by a Neapolitan sixth, *piano*, and the next chord is the dominant in which the G of the previous chord remains as a seventh in the bass.

In the C major section of the beautiful second setting of 'Thekla' the twelfth bar modulates to the tonic minor, and a deceptive cadence passes from the dominant to A flat. Then comes the first inversion of the D flat chord,

and this D flat is suspended as a seventh in the next bar.
The rest of the sentence works its way to C major, so
that although the D flat chord appears to be part of an
A flat phrase it certainly has the effect of a Neapolitan
sixth.

In 'Mignon' I (1821) the chord occurs at the beginning
of the phrase 'sie muss sich erhellen'; but instead of passing to the dominant of B minor it modulates to G major
and turns the opening pathos of the phrase to a beautiful
although momentary serenity. In 'Die Perle' the chord
follows the minor subdominant and is resolved beautifully
in the following progression. (Example 7).

Ex. 7. Die Perle.

The most powerful use of the chord occurs in 'Der
Strom' (Stadler) at 'unmuthig rollt's'. It is *ff* and is
preceded by the chord of A minor and followed by that
of A major in its first inversion. (Example 8).

Ex. 8 Der Strom.

It is a wonderful climax, and on repetition of the line the harmony is altered so that the same chord (of B flat) occurs between those of D minor and B flat minor, the latter then passing to a seventh on C.

The Augmented Sixth

This chord having three forms and therefore at times three chromatic notes, is invaluable for many purposes. It is rich in colour and potentialities and although Schubert generally resolves it in the orthodox manner, its individuality of purpose arouses our delight, and never stales on the ear. How beautiful and apposite it is in the opening of 'Am Meer'; how charmingly placid in 'Widerschein' as 'die Geliebte säumt'[1] and the fisher gazes 'in den Buch und träumt'.[2] In 'Frühlingstraum' it is the harsh crow of the cock, the effect being attained by an unusual resolution of the second inversion of the French sixth below the high E. In the *allegro* section of 'Das Heimweh' (Pyrker) it has a ringing power as it sounds between two tonic chords in A major with the bass leaping up to the minor sixth and down again and thus having no orthodox preparation or resolution. Quite different is it in 'Pause' where it stresses a query and echoes it before the first interlude. The turn to the augmented sixth by enharmonic change on 'Liebespein' is as wonderful as the opening theme of *Tristan,* and the mere alteration in form of the chord on 'Soll' turns it from anguish to the hope that lies hidden in the last line.

[1] *His beloved delays.*
[2] *In the brook and dreams.*

In 'Prometheus' the chord is boldly defiant, crashing in at the end of 'Ich kenne nicht Armeres unter der Sonn', als euch', with the voice alone 'resolving' the chord on 'Götter' before the piano does so: and full of irony at 'dem Schlafenden'. This latter chord on C flat, resolving on to B flat, is followed on the piano by a wider spread augmented sixth that changes to a six-four chord on B flat and then resolves. A somewhat similar change is found in 'An die Leyer'. After the voice has concluded the first recitative the piano breaks on to an angry augmented sixth on C flat resolving to the dominant. After the second recitative the chord on C flat is a diminished seventh falling to the dominant.

The most gloomy use of this chord is in 'Fahrt zum Hades', where 'dem düstern' is ushered in with oppressive gloom. This first stanza is repeated at the end of the song with further additions of the chord in the last line. The line before this reprise ends with the question—'wann?' and here, as in 'Pause' the query is harmonized with the Italian sixth in which the bare augmented fourth in the upper parts opens out on the dominant.

The chord is splendid as a means of modulation or as a passing chord enabling parts to move in close conjunct motion as some of the following examples show.

'Der Neugierige': the modulation from the C major section to that in B major.

'Die Post.' The first stanza closes in D flat. The *ritornello* then modulates by way of the augmented sixth to the original key of E flat, which however does not come to a full close until six bars later.

'Der Flug der Zeit'. The last line but one concludes in
F major. This chord then becomes a German sixth
by the addition of D sharp and the voice goes up
to the major third for 'süsser Ruh'', from C natural
to C sharp at the resolution on a six-four chord in
the original key of A major.

'Die Perle' at the resolution of the E flat in Example
7.

'Der Wanderer' (Schmidt) at the queries 'O Land, wo
bist du?' and 'fragt der Seufzer immer wo'. At the
former we find again the sixth on F natural, and
after its resolution there follows a different chord
on the same bass note F enharmonically changed to
E sharp.

'Memnon': in the seventh and ninth bars. It occurs
also in the tenth bar (as quavers) and passes to the
first inversion of the seventh on C instead of F
minor. The whole of this nine bar sentence is thus
kept gloomy and unresolved until the last lovely
progression to A flat referring to the arrival of
Aurora.

'Orest auf Tauris'. The chord is used quite harshly to
portray the 'starren Felsen, rauhen Waldern'. It
follows a B minor chord, and resolves on a six-four
as the dominant of F sharp minor in which key the
sentence closes. It may be compared with a similar
vocal phrase to 'geistergleich' in 'Auf der Donau'
in which the augmented sixth is treated quite
differently. (Examples 9 and 10).

Ex. 9. Orest auf Tauris

Ex. 10. Auf der Donau.

'Die verfehlte Stunde' (in A flat). The rising emotion reaches a climax as the voice starts the last line on an *fz* augmented sixth, and this chord is repeated *p* to resolve in A flat minor and close in C flat major. The line is then repeated but the piano chord then resolves in A flat major for the final cadence.

'Suleika' II. This is one example of many where the sixth is used as a passing chord. In bars 21-23 it enables the voice to rise from E flat to F by way of E natural as the bass descends G—G flat—F, and the treble rises B flat—C—D.

In 'Trost' it follows a strong discord on 'entschwunden'
with the sixth in the voice part and two bars later it
forms part of the beautiful cadence that gives sad
finality to the last line.

The Dominant Seventh

The Dominant Seventh is so generally used and easily
recognized that only a few examples need be noted. The
seventh is usually included in the cadences because
Schubert loved the fall to the third, and for this purpose
also often used secondary minor sevenths. This falling
seventh provides much of the bright happiness of 'Mein',
especially in the opening stanza.

Sequences of sevenths in some phrases maintain the
pressure on to the final cadence, and sometimes these are
chromatic, with the major third. Such a passage is found
in the tempestuous introduction to 'Der Strom' where
every chord but four is major in the key of D minor.
These are the chords:

D mi./E.E7/A7.D7/G7.C7/D7.G mi./D mi. A/D mi.

Each chord is in the root position with the third or octave
in the treble.

The ecstasy of the conclusion of 'Als ich sie erröthen
sah' is harmonized in a similar manner although here
the treble falls by semitones. The key is G but all the
chords are major triads:

D/B7.E7/A7.D7/G7 C/G7 C/

Another magnificent example concludes 'Aus Heliopolis'
II. The key is C major and the bass falls in thirds from
the tonic but with a passing note at the end of each half

bar which is itself a falling seventh to a major chord (with one exception). The bass is therefore:

C. b flat/A. g F. e/D. c B. a/G

The chord on D is minor, and the last chord is a dominant seventh bringing the sentence back to the opening key.

The Diminished Seventh

Schubert used the diminished seventh more than any other chromatic chord for it is the least certain of them all as its resolution might lead almost anywhere; and it is on resolution that its real significance depends. It generally forms a point of indetermination that may be discovered in any poetic statement. It forms a *sforzando* climax in the second bar of 'Der stürmische Morgen' and its resolution is delayed by the following triplet figure: and it is the frantic cry of 'es ist nichts als der Winter'.

It is at its most tender in 'Der Winterabend' when work has stopped for the day: all is peaceful—'und ist müd' ' (tired). On this phrase the diminished seventh slides into a dominant one for the full close and is echoed in a *ritornello*. This resolution to a minor seventh is common but never stereotyped. It occurs several times in the first page of 'Letzte Hoffnung', and in bar three of 'Der Wegweiser'. It enters into the long chromatic conclusion of the latter song resolving on six-four chords (bars 57, 60, 62 and 71).

One of the most pathetic appearances of this chord is to be found in 'Wasserflut' at the word 'Weh', to which the voice has ascended in a minor scale to the tonic, leading us to expect the normal full close, but the tonic major chord appears as a first inversion with a minor seventh

and then the tonic itself (F sharp) moves up a semitone
to form a diminished seventh. On the resolution of this
chord to the subdominant the voice descends to the lower
tonic with the normal cadence to F sharp minor. This
simple passage of the ascending and descending melodic
minor scale with the *fp* chord as its climax is one of the
many wonders of Schubert's genius for poetic expression
with the most simple material. There are a pair of fierce
diminished sevenths in 'Einsamkeit' (Mayrhofer) at the
opening of the 'Geschwind' in the B flat section, the mere
change in position of the first one being quite startling.
(Example 11).

Ex. 11. Einsamkeit

In 'Trost' there are two strong diminished sevenths in the
penultimate line, one on A flat and the next on A natural,
the latter being altered—piano—to the augmented sixth
noted on p. 55.

In 'An Schwager Kronos' there is a powerful chromatic
passage commencing at 'ergreift im Moore', and in this
whirling series of twenty-three chords there are five
sevenths, five diminished sevenths, six six-four chords,
two augmented sixths, and two diminished fifths formed
by the bass falling a semitone.

E

Example 12 gives the outline reduced to 2/4 from 6/8.

Ex. 12.

It is no haphazard progress for the bass forms definite six-bar phrases below a semi-recitative. It first rises by semitones and then falls to E. This chord is flattened in the bar and commences a phrasing as indicated by the slurs within the last bars which are extended to seven by the enlarged cadence.

The indeterminate character of this chord is well illustrated in two very different songs which use exactly the same notes (F sharp, A, C, E flat). They emerge in bar 3 of 'Auflösung' as a mere shimmer and dissolve

easily into bar 5 as a natural part in the key of G over
a pedal. In 'Die Stadt' they express the misty scene of
damp wind and grey waves, and also the gloomy restless
mind of the poet, all of which is deepened by the tonic
pedal. But the key is C minor in which the diminished
seventh cannot satisfactorily resolve, and hence the coda
of this song does not really 'conclude'.

The Oriental love songs contain many a diminished
seventh although the text books call some of them ninths
and elevenths. In 'Geheimes' every bar except four of the
accompaniment contains two chords one of which—
generally the second—is a discord. Thus the first bar is
tonic to dominant seventh, bar two the same: bar three
is a diminished seventh passing to a minor seventh,
bar four a six-four chord to a diminished seventh, then a
cadence.

'Versunken' has an 'on-running' accompaniment seem-
ing to represent, 'the rippling of the girl's loosened
tresses'.[1] There are many passing notes to confuse the
harmonies, and Capell adds that although the song is in
A flat the opening harmony is the dominant minor ninth
of E flat. Bauer states that it is a dominant minor ninth
over an F minor chord, which further complicates the
solution and still ignores the A flat which would form a
dominant eleventh without a root or third. The most
simple theory is that the chord is a diminished seventh on
F, the D natural being E double-flat and the last of each
four semiquavers being passing notes. This is followed
by a seventh on B flat resolving on E flat, and then the
first two bars are followed by a real sequence a tone

[1] Capell, p. 155.

higher, except for the last chord which is F minor and thus modulates easily into the proper key of A flat as the voice enters. This nomenclature brings the passage in line with Schubert's more general procedure of following diminished sevenths with minor ones on a different root, and reserving the key of the work for a climax.

The aid of the theorists' phantom eleventh may be called in to explain the opening chord of 'Dass sie hier gewesen' in which the top note falls from the eleventh to the tenth and forming what is in fact a diminished seventh, but why not call it that, with an appoggiatura, for it is akin to those in the first part of 'Musensohn'. Indeed much of the song is based on these falling treble notes or, when the chords are inverted, their rising. A charming example from an early work ('Das Heimweh' July 1816) (Example 13) gives us a fairly clear insight into

Ex. 13 Das Heimweh

Schubert's approach to this chord which is so important in the above songs.

It opens on the tonic chord, changes into a sixth on F, and then the A is flattened to form the diminished seventh with B natural, the C being used as a passing note. This is repeated a semitone lower in the next bar and although,

according to theory, the root is C one feels sure that
Schubert had no such note in mind and that therefore
we should accept all such chords as he himself envisaged
them. He released them from their 'dominant discord'
bonds and in this respect at least he produced a new free
chord. We have but to look at some of the diminished
sevenths in 'Prometheus' to see this. As the first part nears
its conclusion there is a chord of A flat. This changes to
a diminished seventh on A natural to usher in the defiant
'Ich kenne nichts Armeres', and even to imagine a C below
the chord would kill the power of this otherwise simple
passage. Then there are the syncopated chords at 'Wer
rettete vom Tode mich' where the A, A sharp, and B are
so obviously the *bass notes*. In contrast to these powerful
outbursts there is the tender use of the chord at 'zu leiden'
on the last page. And as a last example there are the final
lines from 'Der Herbstabend' (1816) where the bass rises
to form these sevenths on the half beats, after an
augmented sixth treated as a seventh and closing inward
on the D natural at 'Kirchhofs Gittern'.

Chromatic Triads

The major chords on the mediant and submediant are
both of frequent occurrence in major and minor keys.
They form an integral part of Schubert's system of bass
progression in thirds. Thus a move from the tonic may
be to mediant or submediant, and either of these may be
used as a pivot for further similar progressions. A simple
example occurs in 'Die Gestirne' where a phrase ends on
C, the dominant of the key. Then the word 'siche' is on
the chord of A major, followed by A flat. The chord in

'Liebeslauschen' might be considered as a dominant of the minor. The key is A major and when the major triad on C sharp (bar 10) occurs it is followed by F sharp minor, and then by the C sharp chord again. Then this is followed by A and the stanza concludes in the opening key. The C sharp chord is thus better considered as a chromatic chord on the mediant. In 'Die abgeblühte Linde' this chord (bar 65) in the same key is resolved on a diminished seventh on C sharp, which proceeds to the chord of D as the subdominant of A.

This observation also applies to 'Sei mir gegrüsst'. These words occur in the song to the chords of G minor and D major. But the key is B flat, and the latter (D major) chord is followed by the full close in the proper key. The final repetitions of the phrase are preceded by an exquisite passage in which the tonality changes from E flat to C flat. The previous passage has closed in E flat and is followed immediately by a major triad a major third lower, and leads on by some beautiful chords to the G minor—D major—F major—B flat major passage of 'sei mir gegrüsst'.

'Der zürnenden Diana' almost immediately proceeds to the major chord on the mediant. It opens with two bars on A flat, and then two on a 'dominant' seventh on C which resolves, not on an F minor chord but a diminished seventh on F which is then flattened to form an augmented sixth and thus back by way of the dominant to A flat. At 'du himmlisch Weib' the chords are A flat, F minor, C major, E flat major to tonic. At the repetition of the words the progression is A flat, F flat, C flat, E flat to tonic, so that there is first a movement downward by a minor third, and then a downward move by a major third. At 'Ich werd' es nie bereuen' there are two descents by a major third, one from the dominant, and one from the tonic to modulate to C flat. This passage concludes by moving up a third to E flat and thence to a section in E major, in which again the major chord on the mediant occurs on 'Schönheit'. In the last A flat section the chord of C again appears, and several bars later ninths and sevenths on the major chord of the submediant, and also two terrific major chords on the leading note.

This song has been quoted rather freely, for although some of the phrases have a semi-modulatory appearance they are really so firmly held in the key itself that they cannot be regarded as outside it. They well illustrate the Schubertian 'swing' in the triad in which three major chords other than tonic, dominant, and subdominant, may be used, sometimes abruptly and at others with chromatic links. They give additional brilliance or passion and are in many cases used so that the voice may bring out an emotional climax on an unexpected major triad. A couple of bars from 'An Laura', which is the twenty-eighth song, clearly illustrates Schubert's sense of their relationship. The key is E major, and below a long E for the voice the chords of A major, C major, and E major are strongly stressed.

An unusual instance occurs at the close of 'Der Winterabend' which is in B flat. The voice ends on the usual full close with the dominant chord at the end of the penultimate bar. The piano then carries on with its accompanying figure but instead of the dominant chord the major chord on the mediant is substituted. This chord is repeated in the next bar and then falls to the tonic (B flat) to form the final cadence.

Schubert's nomenclature is not always theoretically 'correct'. Sometimes a dominant seventh is resolved as an augmented sixth (e.g. 'Sei mir gegrüsst', bar 50) or vice versa. Diminished sevenths, especially, may be written in any sort of way which will make the parts appear to move easily in the harmonic texture unless a startling result is necessary. This is especially so when double sharps or flats would be involved, for these are generally written enharmonically and thus save the reader a lot of trouble although they sometimes make analysis more difficult. But, as mentioned previously, Schubert often considered chords as groups of passing notes and thus wrote each one individually, sharpening those parts that were to rise and flattening those about to fall.

Pedals

These form an integral part of the Schubertian harmony. In some cases they serve merely to keep the original key in the background and in others they form a solid foundation for wild flights of the imagination.

Very many are quite short and may be considered as rather long suspensions in which case they reiterate a definite figure in the accompaniment or enhance the harmony by their delayed movement. They are used occasionally in the vocal line, the outstanding example being at the close of 'Elysium' where the voice holds a top E (the dominant) for seven and a half bars on the first syllable of 'ewig' while the piano quotes an accompanying phrase to a much earlier line, 'Küssen sich auf grünen, sammtnen

Matten'. There is also a long top G in the *lebhaft* section which the voice holds for nine beats while the bass rises chromatically from G up to E flat, and from *p* to *ff*.

The last stanza of 'Der Wegweiser' provides a pedal for the voice, for although the harmonies change, 'Einen Weiser seh' ich stehen *unverrückt*',[1] and the piano emphasizes this on repetition with the eight bars of reiterated tonic. The continual dominant in 'Täuschung' illustrates the 'dancing' light which is after all but the glimmer from a cottage window; and then there is the famous tonic pedal of 'Die Stadt'.

It will be noted that pedals, although common, are used with circumspection for they generally form some part of the harmony even if as part of a strong discord. A typical example of the triplet figure is that of 'Erlkönig', especially at the cry of the child where the dissonances are formed by the voice and the bass moving in thirds below the dominant. Here, and in several other songs, the device is used with great power, but in 'Bertha's Lied in der Nacht' it is used as a murmuring undertone and thus attains a soporific power.

In 'Der Jüngling an der Quelle' a delightful and delicate effect is obtained by the tonic pedal that persists almost throughout the song. It is a dotted minim below the rippling semiquavers and its initial ring and then fading away in each bar gives just the right supporting bass and a piquant touch when dominant harmonies occur.

As the Olympians gather at the beginning of 'Uraniens Flucht' the excitement rises over a long tonic pedal, and in the middle of the song when the anger of Zeus begins

[1] 'One sign I see standing *immovable*'.

to fall there is a dominant pedal on G which at the change of key becomes the third in the chord of E flat.

'Die liebe Farbe' has an ominous dominant pedal held throughout the whole of the vocal part, but it is always an integral part of the harmony except for one passing G natural in the bass. It also plays an important part in the next song, 'Die böse Farbe', but in triplet form. In 'Des Baches Wiegenlied' the bass and treble minims form a kind of double pedal on tonic and dominant, and their accentuation is particularly marked so that they give a suggestion of the passing bell.

The mere mention of bells is sufficient for the introduction of reiterated notes such as the astonishing succession in 'Das Zugenglöcklein'. At 'Horch! des Abendglöckleins Töne'[1] in 'Abendbilder' there are thirty-two minims on the dominant, and in 'Gondelfahrer' the bell of St Mark's sounds the midnight hour, although this is not strictly a pedal as it consists of the chord of the flat submediant struck twelve times. Very often, of course, the bell motiv consists of but one or two notes as in 'Die junge Nonne' and does not come in the category of pedals although very often the harmony changes below or over such notes.

In some cases a pedal is a mere supporting bass such as the bare fifth in 'Der Schmetterling' which accompanies about two-thirds of the lightly tripping upper part with the well-known Schubertian rhythm of a crotchet and two quavers to the bar. 'Auflösung' presents a remarkable case of the pedal being used as a solid foundation for rarely does the bass move from the opening tremolo on

[1] 'Hark! the evening bell sounds'.

the tonic, and even then no more than by a minor third. (See p. 129). The whole of the last forty-four bars of 'Suleika' I is over a lightly tapping dominant pedal: that on the tonic which concludes 'Der Blumen Schmerz' gives a very sombre tone to the passage.

Other important passages could be quoted but we must turn now to what might be considered a miniature pedal which often produces unusual harmonies. It arises from a persistent figure, generally in the bass, and quite often of the pattern so familiar in the first subject of the Unfinished Symphony. It continues throughout 'Abendstern' in the rhythm of the opening bars (Example 14)

Ex. 14. Abendstern

and it will be noted that the tonic bass is maintained below the dominant chord in bar two.

The bass in this and similar songs moves from bar to bar in the usual manner but nearly always the three quavers are the same as the dotted crotchet, and it is above these that passing chords often form unusual harmonies.

'Suleika' I has a similar bass but generally on the dominant, and above the quavers may appear such chords as a six-four or a subdominant chord. In the B flat section of 'Todesmusik' there are reiterated chords over the tonic. The tonic chord changes to a seventh on C, still with a B flat in the treble and bass and the top one then falls to place in the dominant seventh chord (on F), the bass B flat being still maintained and thus retaining its position in the next chord which is the tonic.

'Du liebst mich nicht' and 'Fülle der Liebe' both have the bar rhythm of dotted crotchet and three quavers, and although in the latter the bass moves more freely, yet in both there are occasional strong discords over the reiterated bass. It sometimes occurs in four-four time as in 'Der Zwerg' where it has a most ominous effect as the harmonies keep shifting from tonic to dominant above the three quavers. This 'miniature pedal' may thus form an important 'motiv', or it may provide a point of stability in a sort of quicksand of emotion and by so doing heighten the tension by underlying the symbolizing of what might be with the suggestion of the inescapable and implacable reality.

V

MODULATION

AMID the many and varied forms of modulation
Schubert still had a place for the most common of them.
In many songs there is a simple turn to the dominant or
subdominant, or to the major or minor: and in some
there is no modulation at all. Often there is merely the
suggestion of a change, like that in 'Schweizerlied',
which although it keeps to the key of F, has a kind of
false cadence to the second phrase where the third and
fifth of the tonic are chromatically retarded, G sharp and
B natural rising a semitone to A and C above the bass.
So in the 'Wiegenlied' ('Schlafe') in A flat, the second
phrase commences on the dominant as though to
modulate, and although it does not do so, the little deceit
is maintained by the B flat at the end of the phrase rising
to the C of the final A flat phrase by way of B natural,
as though it were 'modulating' back again.

In 'An die Natur' the first four bars are in F and the
next four hover between G and C, and the last two are
in F again. This is one of Schubert's favourite forms in
the short songs. He likes to get the modulation near the
end, or even at the end, in which case he repeats the last
line in the opening key. 'Heidenröslein' in G, modulates
to D, and then returns for the short refrain of the last
two lines. It is rather surprising to find that all the

cadences in 'An die Musik' are in the tonic except for
the last line which is in the relative minor, after which
it is repeated in the home key. In 'Das Wandern' the
modulation to the dominant would also be quite near
the end of the song but for the four repetitions of the
refrain—'das Wandern'.

It is in these songs, so simple at first glance, that we
see the intimate connection between modulation and
form. There is always such diversity that we can never
be sure what turn the melody will take or into what key
the harmonies will sprout. In 'Des Müllers Blumen' the
first cadence is on the dominant E, but although the bass
E is approached via D sharp there are D naturals in the
melody. However the repetition of the sentence has an
altered ending with the new leading note in the melody
and a full close cadence so that it is *in* the dominant this
time, and then a simple but charming little modulation
leads back to A.

The same procedure is followed in 'Thränenregen' (in
A); the first four bars close on the dominant, the next
four *in* it. But this is only half the song. The next four
bars close on the chord of C sharp major and we see the
significance of the inner part of the opening chords—that
intrusive E sharp which now forms a definite part of the
new cadence. The last stanza is in the minor and only
modulates back in the last line on a tender 'Ade', but even
then the coda is half in the major and half in the minor.
'Mit dem grünen Lautenbande' modulates once, and on
the penultimate line into the dominant. The phrase 'an
der Wand' has been explained on p. 34, and the same
notes are harmonized diatonically a few bars later at

'heut' zu mir'. A further surprise meets us in 'Morgen-gruss'. First there are the intrusive C and F sharps in the key of C and then for the middle section a most delightful sequence of alternate minor and major chords with the bass and melody falling in thirds to the dominant cadence at the fermata.

The last song in this cycle modulates as one might expect to the subdominant, but its more sombre tone is accentuated by the fact that the previous line 'du bist zu Haus' closes on the major chord of the mediant, leading us to expect the relative minor. Hence the phrase 'Die Treu' ist hier' with its D naturals becomes, although in the major, most pathetic; and the final lines do seem to linger in the minor merely because whenever the mediant occurs in the melody it is supported by the submediant chord.

The most characteristic modulation is the sudden change to the mediant or submediant key. It is interesting to note that although Beethoven modulated little in most of his songs there are several examples of what Bauer calls *Terz-modulationen*. One is a minor third down, another a major third down, and there are two each of the minor and major third up. The Schubert examples are much too numerous to catalogue and only a few can be quoted to show the important purpose they serve. This purpose is linked with that noted in the examination of those chromatic chords referred to as the 'swinging triad' (p. 63). Two famous songs may be cited to illustrate this: 'Der Musensohn' with its alternating sections in G and B, and 'Nacht und Träume' at the change from B to G. In both cases the reason for the modulation is obvious.

In the former the B is heard so often in the voice part in the G major section that it is hardly recognized for the moment as the new tonic, and then at the end of the B major section it is suddenly transmuted again to a major third. In the latter song the tonic B is also repeated by the voice as it takes up the mediant of the new key. This indeed is the usual method of such modulation, its object being to express a tender ecstasy of feeling, as the last note in one key becomes the mediant in the next.

In 'Der gute Hirte' the first section ends in E with the voice on the fifth of the chord. This B is then repeated above the chord of G major for the beautiful passage 'Er weidet mich', and the new key is emphasized in a very delicate manner by the following chord which is the second inversion of the dominant seventh, thus introducing another 'accidental' in the melody, and again bringing the new mediant into the foreground as the seventh falls. A similar progression occurs in 'An den Mond in einer Herbstnacht'. The first sentence is in A major and the voice concludes on the mediant, but the following *ritornello* modulates to E major. The key then changes immediately to C major with the voice taking up the E as a new mediant for 'Leis' sind deine Tritte'. The opposite effect occurs in another important Schreiber song 'Das Abendroth'. After a glowing address to the setting sun the piano carries on with its figuration to a full close in E major. The next section opens solemnly with the line 'Des Aufgangs Berge still und grau', and although the voice commences on the mediant of E major for the first word, its repetition on the next syllable is accompanied by the chord of C sharp minor

Wilhelm Müller

Johann Rudolf Zumsteeg

Friedrich von Matthisson   Johann Mayrhofer

Franz von Schober

in which key the passage remains for a few bars until the beautiful modulation back to the relative major at the words 'hellen Gluthen'.

This form of modulation first occurs in the twelfth, thirteenth and twenty-fifth songs at the beginning of 1814. The first is in the very long song 'Der Taucher' where a passage ending in C major turns to A flat for the entry—'Und ein Edelknecht'. The next is in 'Don Gay-seros' I in which each section modulates to a subdominant until the key of B is reached, from which there is a sudden skip to G. The third is 'Adelaide', which is in A flat, where the third stanza enters. There is a short modulation to G flat and this in turn changes to E flat minor, thus producing a three-bar sequence. Mayrhofer's 'Am See' (December 1814) is the first striking example. The recitative:

> *Ein Strahlenbild schwebt mir voran,*
> *Und muthig wag' ich's Leben dran*[1]

has the first line in E flat, but the second crashes out *fortissimo* on a B major chord to modulate to that key.

The other modulations in the early stages are of little interest because they have no special significance except when they are the major-minor form. They add variety and give point to some of the sections but they do not have the inevitability that seems so obvious in all the later songs.

Thus we find his most characteristic modulation used with purpose in 1814 and its occurrence very frequent

[1] *A glowing vision sweeps me on,*
I dauntless dare my life thereon.

F

right up to the last song, for in the second stanza of 'Die Taubenpost' it stands out at 'Kein Briefchen' as the first word is on the octave of D major and the next on the third of B flat; and in the last stanza there is a modulation from G to C and then from C to A. As the song is in the key of G the former example may be taken as the triad swing of the chords G, B flat and D.

The 'weit, hoch, herrlich' passage in 'An Schwager Kronos' is famous. Starting from E flat it passes to the chord of B major as the dominant of E minor which changes to C major. This becomes a dominant seventh to F minor which passes to D flat. This is written enharmonically as C sharp major and leads by way of F sharp minor and B minor to the dominant of the D major section. This produces a sequence of E flat—B : E—C : F —C sharp. It will also be noted that the first D major section closes on its dominant and is followed by F major thus dropping a third from A to F (at 'Labe'), and then modulating a third lower for the D minor 'reprise' of the opening eight bars. The sudden modulations in 'Die Sterne' (Leitner) are all in thirds—from E flat to C and back again, then to C flat and back; and then to G and back. 'Hark, hark, the lark' (in C) goes straight from the chord of G to that on E flat to lead to A flat, and then that key note is used as the bass of an augmented sixth to lead back to the original key. There are so many examples of this form of modulation that it is a wonder they do not become stereotyped. Bauer lists over fifty and this number could easily be doubled, but they are so apposite and so often unexpected that their charm disguises their similarity.

Unfortunately we have no name for this kind of modulation. It is in form enharmonic for its effect is to alter the character of a note. When, for example, the D major sections of 'Das Lied im Grünen' change to B flat the voice maintains the D in each chord. There is no alteration in the note itself but its new environment gives it quite a different aspect. It has changed from a tonic to a mediant, and this is the whole value of the procedure for by such means a note in any key may become quite another in relationship to its new surroundings, and it was because Schubert concentrated on the mediant so often that these modulations had to move up or down in major or minor thirds.

In addition to this sudden modulation there are the contrasts of 'thirds' brought about by means of the modulatory passage. How delightful is the four-bar modulation from B to G in 'Liebesbotschaft', and the manner in which the E major section of 'Die Erwartung' slips into its relative minor and then later into the key of G at 'und alle Wesen seh' ich Wonnetauschen', and the sudden change from the chord of F to D, for 'und scherzt und spielt' which is after all only a brief modulation from B flat to its relative minor ! In 'Atys' the section 'Ich liebe' opens in F and the first sentence closes on the dominant and then modulates to D flat by resolving the dominant seventh on that chord, and a few bars later a similar change is made by a dominant seventh on B flat to C flat.

There are several such modulations in 'Einsamkeit' (Mayrhofer) which can easily be identified. The first is from B flat to F sharp, then A flat to E, and A to F. This latter, like several other such cases, is really from a dominant of one key to the tonic of another, because the previous passage is in D but closes on its dominant so that the key of F is related in thirds in either case. The problem of classification therefore depends on whether it is the contrast of two passages in different keys, or the chords immediately concerned in the modulation that is the more important. Thus when a passage in D is followed by one in F there is a rise of a minor third, but if the first closes on its dominant A in a decisive manner there the change of tonality must be looked upon as a major third down. On the other hand, if the section in F opens on its dominant of C from the previous close on A there is a further move upward of a minor third. The permutations possible are therefore many in number and it is because Schubert makes full use of them that his modulations by this method always have an element of surprise and add to the emotional content of the verse by their skilled manipulation. They could be neatly tabulated by adhering to the definition of modulation quoted elsewhere, but this would not be of great value for it is the intent of the passage and not its nomenclature that concerns us. When there is a change of key it is not so often for the relationship *per se* as for the effect involved by this change. Therefore our chief attention should be directed to the two or three bars concerned, and if there is a change from a chord on G to one on B major then that is the first consideration, to be followed, if necessary, by attention to the origin of the first chord and the progression of the second.

There is also little doubt that these chromatic chords

and triad modulations were associated in Schubert's mind with the Neapolitan chord, which enharmonically contains the sharpened tonic and dominant. Therefore although the Neapolitan sixth is an easily accepted part of diatonic harmony it contains two notes which are as far from the original key as possible, one becoming enharmonically the major third on the submediant and the other the major third on the mediant. Hence the many various Schubertian progressions may range over these changes from the most elusive to the most startling effects.

Modulation to an adjacent key is more often by a semitone than a tone, one reason for this being that Schubert often used the triad on the flattened supertonic, and could also consider the tonic triad itself in that position. Here again it is difficult to distinguish between modulation to a chord and to a key. Thus in 'Stimme der Liebe' (in D) the first sentence closes in A flat. This becomes enharmonically G sharp and the leading note to the chord of A—hence a modulation up a semitone. But the next chord of A becomes a dominant seventh to key D minor which modulates down to B flat. Four bars later the bass B flat moves up to C flat as the lower note of a diminished seventh the upper notes of which fall to form the triad on B (C flat)—another rising semitone modulation.

'Die Erwartung' supplies some very interesting cases. For example the *recit.* 'Rief es von ferne' leads from the previous key of E flat to that of E. This it does by opening with a beautiful phrase in B flat to symbolize the circles made by the swan on the lake; repeats it in G and then closes in F which passes in a delightful manner to B major as the dominant of E: thereby producing the inner contrast between B flat and B (which has a *fermata*) and the outer one of E flat and E. 'Liebesbotschaft' is a parallel case. The second stanza closes in C but eight bars later the key of B is prominent, and it is approached by sequence thus:

chords of 1st line of third stanza
> A minor. E. E minor. G minor. D.

chords of 2nd line of third stanza
> F (major). C. — A minor. B.

Modulation by a tone up or down is of course closely associated with sequence, one brief example occurring in 'Danksagung an den Bach, at the line 'Zur Müllerin hin, so lautet der Sinn' to the chords of A 7 to D and G 7 to C and the following 'Hab' ich's verstanden' (twice) on G sharp 6 to A minor and F sharp 6 to G.

The famous modulation from B to C in 'Der Neugierige' (after 'Ja, heisst das—') need only be mentioned here. It is simple and startling. There is a similar modulation in 'Todesmusik'. A passage closes in B major and the following line, 'Alles Schöne, das mir blühte', is on a Neapolitan sixth but a few following bars remain in the key of C major before going further afield into B flat. This section concludes on a full close which is followed by the chord of B flat minor, and this is then enharmonically changed to A sharp major to lead to the last page in G!

The 'Ossian' songs being so free in form and so full of recitative depend largely on harmonic illustration, and many striking modulations may be found therein. In 'Der Tod Oscars' the line 'Meine Augen sind von Thränen erblindet' commences in A flat and closes in C flat with a very pathetic effect as the voice takes the falling fifth on the G flat dominant seventh. It is marked *mit Schmerz*, and a passage near the end is directed *Mit letzter Kraft*, having powerful full bar chords of E major, C major, and a third inversion of the seventh on D passing to the dominant seventh of E minor. 'Cronnan' also has many fine passages. One leads to the chord of A flat minor. This is a first inversion and the bottom C flat becomes B as the chord changes enharmonically to the dominant seventh of the following section in E major. Later on the key changes from A flat to C minor merely by turning the former chord into an augmented sixth resolving to G.

Some changes of key are so abrupt that they can hardly be called modulations. In 'Uranians Flucht' she exclaims 'Ich bin's!' on a seventh on B flat in the treble and this is followed by the seventh on B natural in the bass to lead to the key of E. In the middle of her narration there is a full close on G flat, followed immediately by E flat for a section in that key. This closes finally on G flat again, followed by a scale passage over a pedal G. Later, when her anger dissolves in tears there is a beautiful modulation from A flat minor to E, the voice passing enharmonically from A flat to G sharp with the change of key made one beat earlier in the vocal line than in the accompaniment.

In 'Kriegers Ahnung' the first part closes on the dominant of C minor and passes immediately to A flat major.

Then follows a close on D flat which undergoes an enharmonic change to C sharp that in the piano part might be taken to be in the key of A. However the voice rises to F sharp on 'düst'rer Schein' and thus 'clouds' the chord into F sharp minor. A beautiful harmonic passage ensues in which a gradual change is made to A minor by the flattening of one note at a time. There is then a modulation to F minor and the Neapolitan sixth is used momentarily as a phrase in G flat major. There is also a most touching turn at the end of the *Geschwind* section at 'Herzliebste, gute Nacht', the second syllable being on C minor and closing in A flat which becomes an augmented sixth to lead to the coda in C minor.

The second stanza of 'Aufenthalt' closes in B minor. In the *ritornello* the piano accentuates this close by repeating it over the bass E, E sharp, F sharp, B, and then repeats the four bars but with a bass of E, E flat, D and G which throws into relief the middle subject in the relative major. A somewhat similar process occurs in 'Ihr Bild'. The first stanza opens in B flat minor and closes in B flat major. The *ritornello* strengthens the major sense by echoing the bass of 'Heimlich zu leben begann' (which is a minor phrase) in the treble a third higher and thus with a major interval. The effect of the following stanza in G flat major is hence much enhanced. As the third stanza is the same as the first and closes in the tonic major it is followed by a pathetic variant of the ritornello which is now in the minor.

Such masterly simplicity abounds in these last songs that many beautiful details are apt to be overlooked or accepted without a second thought. Not only are there slight variations in the second stanza of 'Das Fischer-mädchen' which is a minor third higher than the first and third, but the manner in which the key is introduced and left is most beautiful. The first *ritornello* is like the prelude except for the subtle insertion of an F flat which turns the harmonies to C flat: then in the bar before the third stanza the F flat is followed in the next chord by F natural to bring about the simple but magic return to A flat. The many delicate nuances in this song raise it far above all the other Schubert barcarolles, fine as many of them are. There is the simple modulation to the tonic minor at 'komm zu mir' and the return as the piano breaks into a little melody a sixth below 'wir Kosen Hand in Hand', and at the second repetition of this line, falls from G flat to F and then rises by way of G natural to A flat.

VI

EXPRESSION MARKS
AND GRACE NOTES

EXPRESSION marks are relative to tempo, volume and mood, and if Schubert was at times sparing in his directions it was only because he thought the true feeling inherent in word and music should be obvious to the interpreter. The usual marks of volume of sound are used and range from *ppp* to *fff*, but they may be still further stressed by such directions as *mit aller Kraft* or *mit halbe Stimme, sehr leise* or *stark*.

Sometimes however the volume is changed merely by an alteration in the accompaniment, a beautiful example of which is found in 'An die Freunde'. It opens *pp* and in the first stanza the voice is accompanied only by a slow staccato-stepping bass. Then the key changes to the tonic major for 'Und wann die Erde sich verjüngt',[1] and to prevent the singer bursting forth like the Spring another *pp* is inserted, for this change is brought about not only by the new key but by the blossoming forth of the harmony with a counter-melody. There is only one other mark, which is an important *fp* on 'alles'. It is therefore important to observe the form of the music for interpretation of volume. It is obvious that full harmonies must sound louder than two simple lines of treble and

[1] When Spring returns.

bass and that strong discords have more penetrating power than simple triads; but the scale of values is different for widely differing types of song. For example, the *forte* in the delicate outline of 'Seligkeit' is not equal to that in 'Die Allmacht'.

Signs not often met with are *accelerando* and *rallentando*, but this is because Schubert in so many cases incorporated such movement in his phrases, a few instances of which have already been mentioned in Chapter II. Song endings provide some other interesting examples. 'Wohin' concludes with 'fröhlich nach' repeated three times, the last being all on the dominant with a long final note.[1] The last line of 'Morgengrüss' is treated in a similar manner with a whole bar note to the first syllable of 'gehen', and in both these cases we have a clear rallentando without alteration of tempo. In several of the last songs there are very impressive examples. 'Liebe' in 'Liebesbotschaft' occupies two whole bars on repetition instead of the half bar previously used: note also the final words of 'Frühlingssehnsucht' and 'Ständchen'.

'In der Ferne' produces two varieties of this prolongation of phrase. The first two stanzas repeat their last lines of two bars in a five bar phrase over prolonged chords ending with a *fermata*, but in the following stanzas there is not this big effect of *ritenuto* because the accompaniment urges the rhythm on irresistibly below the long vocal phrase and there is no *fermata*. An

---

[1] Many singers slow down at the end of this song because they have not realized that the final monotone achieves this result by contrast with the previous phrases.

accelerando is marked towards the end of 'Der Doppel-gänger' and this is not contradicted later because the phrasing has a big retarding effect: whereas the penulti-mate line occupies barely two bars the last line is practic-ally three times as long. (To be exact the ratio is five and a half beats to fifteen beats).

Although Schubert used the usual Italian musical terms in his instrumental music he used German in nearly all the songs, and it is of interest to note when he commenced this procedure. He did not follow Zumsteeg's example in this, for the first twenty-two songs are nearly all with Italian terms. German is first used in 'Klaglied' but in the next song both languages are used, and in 'Der Taucher' there is one German term amid various Italian ones. 'Adelaide' is wholly in German and the next nine songs in Italian.

The Matthisson songs of July 1814 have Italian terms but those of September and onwards have German indications, and as 'Adelaide' is dated only 1814 it may have been composed in the autumn with the later songs, which would bring the general use of German as com-mencing on 17 September 1814. Therefore it seems evident that by that time Schubert felt he had broken with the Italian tradition and was producing indigenous songs and only rarely did he depart from this method.

The terms used are of great variety, and as about a hundred German words occur they must form in various combinations nearly two hundred phrases of tempo and expression. The latter are profuse and include such terms as *düster, unschuldig, mit heilige Rührung, erzählend, scherzhaft* and so on, many of which had never before been applied to music and would have been unintelligible at that time if indicated in Italian.

It is in terms of speed and quality that misjudgement sometimes occurs. The former are confined chiefly to *Langsam*, *Mässig*, and *Geschwind* or *Schnell* with such qualifications as *sehr*, *etwas* or *ziemlich*. There are only eight songs which open *schnell*, and twelve *geschwind*, so that the number of really fast songs is very limited. One of the fastest passages occurs in 'Lied des Orpheus', for after the *ziemlich langsam* section comes *geschwind*, four bars later *geschwinder werdend* and then on the next page *geschwinder*.

In considering the speed of a song the words themselves are of prime importance for unless they are heard clearly the whole musical structure falls to the ground. To ensure this in a quick tempo Schubert writes the notes for the voice in broad phrases and those of the accompanying figure are short. Note the broad melody of 'Erlkönig' against the triplet pedal, or the dotted crotchets in 'Der Strom' against the semiquavers of the piano. But there is more to it than this. Quickly reiterated chords may add excitement but do not create speed, and it is by the varied figuration of the chords and the onward-surging harmonies that Schubert achieves this. Only in Italian does he write an *allegro vivace* such as that in 'Il modo di prender moglie' in which the vocal line consists of quavers.

The one important exception is 'Der Jäger' which is generally taken much too fast.[1] It is marked *geschwind* but it is evident that this refers to the quaver notes and

[1] Capell, p. 55, says it 'is rushed into nonsense'.

not to the duple beats. The songs first published under the opus numbers 1 to 7 were given metronome marks (except Op. 2), and as presumably Schubert had some hand in this we have a general guide to his ideas of tempi. Here are a few:

Tempo	Time	Title	M.M.
Erlkönig	Schnell	C ♩	=152
Rastlose Liebe	Schnell	3/4 ♩	=152
Drang in die Ferne	etwas geschwind	9/8 ♩.	= 76
			(a later work)
Der Fischer	mässig	2/4 ♩	= 60
Schäfers Klagelied	mässig	6/8 ♪	=120
Morgenlied	ziemlich langsam	₵ ♩	= 63
Der König in Thule	etwas langsam	2/4 ♩	= 66
Wanderers Nachtlied	langsam	C ♩	= 50
Erster Verlust	sehr langsam	₵ ♩	= 54
Jägers Abendlied	sehr langsam	2/4 ♪	= 63
Meeres Stille	sehr langsam	₵ ♩	= 72

Examination of the verses of these songs will show that due regard to the words has been considered and that Schubert is as likely to take a half beat as a beat for his standard. Neglect of this point has led to several dubious interpretations which have now become practically orthodox and it would be as well for singers to reconsider these matters and strike out boldly on new lines if necessary. 'Nacht und Träume', like 'Meeresstille' is *sehr langsam* but it always rendered very much slower. The style of accompaniment does indicate a slower tempo but not about half speed. Schubert did not write the work as an exercise in breath control; nor did he use *alla breve* as an indication of double speed. Hence there is a tempo relationship between the two songs.

'Der Musensohn' is a song that is taken too fast because of a misunderstanding of the direction *ziemlich lebhaft*. The latter word is a term of mood, not speed, for liveliness or animation does not entail velocity although it denotes vivacity. It has come, like the Italian *vivace*, to intimate a speed, but Schubert did not use it in this manner as is shown by other indications. A section of 'Elysium' is marked *Lebhaft, geschwind* and the latter word would not have inserted if the former had been used to indicate speed. So in 'Lob des Tokayers' the indication *Nicht zu geschwind doch lebhaft* clearly shows the distinction between speed and mood.

There are seven songs marked merely *lebhaft*, the most important of which is 'Die Berge' (Schlegel); and of the three *etwas lebhaft* one is 'Die Knabe in der Wiege'. 'Der Musensohn' is the only song *ziemlich lebhaft*, and an indication that means 'fairly lively' does not suggest that the son of the muses is racing through the country-side at breakneck speed. He is happy and gay but his music has a dancing lilt for the lads and lasses: and as to tempo it is a jolly *ländler* rather than a tarantella.

Grace Notes

These are many and varied and are not ornamental but additional means of expression, being often written out instead of indicated by the usual signs because they depart from the accepted forms. The mordent adds brightness to the opening sentence of 'Frühlingstraum' but it is doubtful whether the voice should perform the phrase in the same manner. Its quality in bar five of 'Gute Nacht' is indefinable but its significance is easily observed by playing the phrase with, and then without it. It is written out in the second half of the stanzas in 'Ständchen' (Rellstab) and several other songs; and in 'Hippolit's Lied' it occurs twice in nearly every bar, and as it is on a note always followed by the semitone below it is in effect a variant of the turn.

The trill is never[1] used for the voice and seldom in the accompaniment, although it is an important figure in 'Freiwilliges Versinken' and Schlegel's 'Abendröthe.' It also illustrates the spinning 'Wetterfahne' and is written out in full as the background music of 'Im Dorfe'.

The turn is very frequently used, especially at cadences and as it generally forms a very significant part of the phrase it is most often written out with some variant. In 'Der Doppelgänger' there is first the plain phrase 'wohnte mein Schatz', then at 'auf demselben Platz' it has a turn, and finally there is the turned phrase of 'in alter Zeit?' The turns that conclude 'Die Allmacht' and 'Am Meer' are the same except that the B in the latter is dotted. In 'Gesänge des Harfners' I (Op. 12) the turns are triplets with an initial appoggiatura: in II there is one written out on 'Mächte' and one indicated in the usual way eight bars later.

Its value as part of the melody, especially in order to enhance the mediant, is obvious in many a song. The ends of the first and second phrases of 'An die Musik' are really turns on the supertonic, and in 'Am Grabe

[1] Well, hardly ever! There is a trill in the short cadenza to 'Der Hirt auf dem Felsen'.

Johann Gabriel Seidl

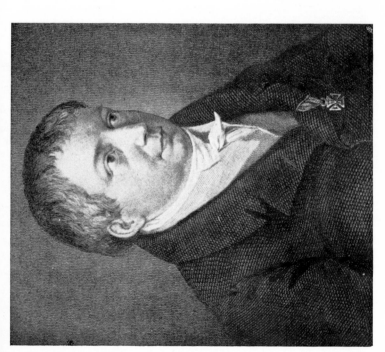

Friedrich von Schlegel

Hedwig von Staegemann—the original of Die schöne Müllerin

Anselmos' there is a similar beautiful cadence at the
mention of the beloved name, with a most expressive
harmonic progression from G flat to B flat via A flat. In
Schreiber's 'An den Mond' a turn on the subdominant
consists of four semiquavers. In the introduction the first
note is tied to the previous chord: it springs up from
the tonic on the first syllable of 'Antlitz': and later, at
'wiederkehren' its first two notes belong to the first
syllable and the last two take the second syllable.

From an almost endless variety of turns that from
Rellstab's 'Ständchen' may be quoted as being of special
interest because it is an addition to an 'ornament'
already present. In the first part of the song the vocal
phrases commence on a triplet with a rise and fall, but
at 'in des Mondes Licht' the triplet is reversed and the
rise indicated by a pair of grace notes thus making a
turn of five notes. Then there is the last phrase of 'Atlas'
where the A flat, G, and F sharp are but a turn on the
upper tonic and raised by its phrasing and accentuation
to a powerful degree.

If the appoggiatura is also considered as of additional
significance rather than as a mere ornament certain
difficulties in interpretation will disappear. The practice
of deleting the first of two similar notes when it is
preceded by the appoggiatura is questionable, especially
when it is considered that of two similar phrases in 'Die
Stadt' one has the grace note while the other is written
out in full.[1] One point to note is that the first occurs
on the third syllable of 'Horizonte' while the latter is
on the first syllable of 'einmal'. In 'Prometheus' the

[1] Capell, p. 254.

G

appoggiaturas (before the first of two notes of the same pitch) are on the words 'Sonne', 'droben', '(er)-barmen', 'deine'; in 'An die Leyer' they are on 'singen', 'tauschen', 'schreiten' 'rauschen'.

It will be noted that they are nearly always on a syllable commencing with a consonant, and often an explosive one, thereby not only giving verbal inflection but accentuating the word involved. The word 'Schnee' in 'Erstarrung' has an appoggiatura and is therefore sung with two notes on the third beat, and the first half of 'meinem' four bars later, although followed by the same note, should surely be performed in the same manner. As in the latter half of 'Gefror'ne Thränen', the grace note on 'wolltet' leaps from the E flat to A natural giving two notes for the first beat, why should the same pattern not be followed in the phrase 'Ei Thränen'?

There is a similar pattern in 'Danksagung an den Bach' at 'Singen'—'Klingen', and all the evidence seems to prove that when Schubert wrote an appoggiatura he meant it to be performed as such. Perhaps some confusion has been caused by relating the voice too closely to the accompaniment. In 'Einsamkeit' the word 'ruhig' is on two similar notes (A natural) with an appoggiatura to the first of these, and as this is echoed on the piano by two notes only there is an inclination to sing the word in the same way by cutting out the first A. The second sentence of 'Der greise Kopf' concludes in a similar manner with an appoggiatura before the first of two notes on G, but in the following *ritornello* the whole phrase is repeated with a crotchet suspension on the A. But that it is no pattern for the vocal line is proved by the first sentence which has two mordents while the following piano phrase omits the first of these and substitutes a turn for the second. In fact there are many songs in which the *ritornelli* are varied slightly and cannot therefore be taken as interpretations of the voice part.

As one further justification for singing all such phrases as written it is only necessary to call attention to the very many cases in which the first syllable in a bar has two notes, as in 'Der Jüngling am Bache' and the second part of 'Der Müller und der Bach', or two syllables occur close together as in the opening of 'Kriegers Ahnung'. Such phrasing is characteristic of Schubert so there should be no hesitation in singing appoggiaturas in the same manner.

Nevertheless there are some anomalies which raise the question as to why Schubert used these grace notes at all. He shows no reluctance in writing suspensions and discords on a strong beat in ordinary notation in so very many instances that it is very curious that he should resort to the appoggiatura in as many others. In 'Gefror'ne Thränen', in the A flat section, the word 'Brust' is on a dominant seventh (D flat) with an appoggiatura. It would therefore seem to be similar in pattern to bar sixteen although this is written out in quavers in spite of the discord of the first note of 'ich'. It may be that the preliminary note on 'Brust' is an acciaccatura, but this is not in keeping with the other similar phrases.

From these various observations there seem to be two conclusions. The first is that this grace note is used for the purpose of accentuation. When a phrase is to run smoothly it is written out in full, but where a stress is

to fall on the first of two notes the appoggiatura is used
(c.f. 'einkehren' and 'Wandrer' in 'Das Wirthshaus'.)
Even this is subject to exceptions for some phrases that
fall in the latter group are written in ordinary notes with
an accent mark over the first note, and the amount of
stress in either case can only be calculated by the context;
and from this the second conclusion arises which is that
the length of the appoggiatura is indeterminate. The
interpretation must depend, as previously emphasized,
on the context, and the duration of the leaning note
adjusted accordingly.[1]

[1] 'Schubert', writes Capell, 'did not as a rule trouble to make
his notation plain on this point, and the singer has to form his
own judgement whether the appoggiatura is "crushed" or is
weightier than the note on which it leans'.

VII

THE SCHUBERT IDIOM[1]

IN dealing with the technique of the songs in the previous chapters an attempt has been made to realize the purpose of some of the various devices that combine to form the Schubert idiom. It has been noted that he kept generally within the usual recognized bounds of form and harmony. He was quite capable of expressing himself in the musical vocabulary of his time, although he very often deviated from what may be called standard practice, and it is possible to discuss the music from these two points of view. So far we have been concerned chiefly with the variations and deviations in technique, each of which serves a purpose, as for instance the case in which a song concludes in a key different from its commencement, the expressive value of a modulation, and the chromatic chord that gives point to a phrase.

Hence part of the individuality in Schubert's music resides in these factors the ramifications of which have been shown to centre largely on the major third, for in so very many cases the mediant occupies such a prominent place that it may be said to dominate Schubert's melodies. It is when we consider the melodies themselves that analysis fails to a large extent for there

[1] See also a general survey of Schubert's music under this title by T. C. L. Pritchard in the Symposium.

is no standard of comparison owing to the fact there is so much more individuality in a tune than in an harmonic progression. Even though the perfect cadence always consists of the same two chords the number of possible variations in the vocal phrase above it is very large indeed, and although harmony and melody are really an inseparable unit it is by the tunefulness of the vocal writing that the songs are best known.

It is the ingenuous character of many of Schubert's melodies that has caused them to be accepted at face value only. He, like Handel and Haydn, often put on paper the uninhibited thoughts that carry a sense of careless rapture which is foreign to their three great contemporaries and which still meets with some criticism in Schubert's case. But despite the trend of modern music the general concensus of opinion is (and will probably remain) that a song must have a good melody. If it is to be widely accepted with pleasure it must be written in the vulgar tongue of music, for beauty conforms much more to recognized standards than it deviates from them. But a good melody has a content far beyond that of mere beauty which as an abstract entity can have no place in a song, for it is only when the melodic outline, the form of accompaniment and the rhythm of the sentences as expressed by a progression of harmonies are attuned in perfect union with the poetry that a song may be considered ideal. The melody itself has a hidden significance that cannot be analyzed but which the mind perceives with intense satisfaction because each rising and falling interval stirs memories buried deep in our heritage of emotions, and therefore the curve of a melody carries little meaning unless its movement conforms to such unconscious patterns, which are so involved and so sensitive to minute variations that the composer may stir us deeply with a quite simple arrangement of notes and excite us by a simple rearrangement.

We are consciously aware of but a few of these sound effects and responses. The most common is the rising fourth so often found as an anacrusis, and deviations from this—especially the rising major sixth—have been noted previously. Schubert avoids the rising fourth in the conclusion of 'Prometheus' at 'Hier sitz' ich' in order to accentuate the falling octave of the second and third words; and no passage is more striking than the opening of the finale of 'Gruppe aus dem Tartarus' where 'Ewigkeit' bursts forth in C major with no anacrusis. It is true that the words do not allow for this, but Schubert has made the most of the opportunity provided by purposely (or even unconsciously) commencing the previous phrases, from 'Fragen sich', on a weak beat and phrasing the two bars of interlude after 'Vollendung sei?' in the same manner and then stopping the rhythm (but not the pulsation) in the *crescendo* bar before 'Ewigkeit'. Hence the electrifying effect, which is ruined in those English translations which substitute 'Eternity' and insert an anacrusis.

Other obvious effects are falling and rising phrases, various examples of which will occur to the reader, and the falling minor phrase that conveys melancholy or even dread as in 'Die Krähe', the first bar of which bears the foreboding atmosphere associated with the crow of folk-legend, and which merely by inversion served

Wagner for the uninhibited outburst of gaiety in the first act of *Tristan* at the sailors' chorus. This is a small but excellent example of the inherent emotional content of a phrase, but it is impossible to analyse the various possible effective permutations involved in a simple diatonic passage and hence we say that a composer's melody is inspired for he could not possibly calculate all the combinations of the chromatic scale even if he were consciously aware of the effects they must produce in the mind of the auditor.

He must form his melody by an instinctive sense of right feeling, and once it has arisen in his mind he can only alter minor details, for if he reshapes it to any extent it loses its depth of significance. This is one reason for the large number of fragments and variants in the Deutsch Catalogue. Some works were commenced and then abandoned because of dissatisfaction, and others were started afresh and brought to a successful conclusion on different lines; but the most interesting cases are those in which only minor details have been altered. They are minor only in size, not in significance. One of the most important and well-known occurs in the first subject of the C major symphony in which a G is altered to D. The original version is characterless as an opening subject and yet reminiscent of greatness. Perhaps Schubert noticed its similarity to the opening figure of the Adagio of Beethoven's Fourth Symphony, in which it is of vital import: but more probably he detected its lack of urgency. His first subject as a whole is a soaring one and merely by the alteration of a note he welds the first four bars together so that the wind instruments, with their arpeggios on bassoon and horn, complete what might be considered as the first attempted lift to flight on the part of the strings. Thus does a slight adjustment become a major revolution and a good many similar instances may be found in the songs, for although Schubert wrote so quickly because his mind responded so speedily to the poem he had examined he often found the need for slight revision.

Quite often, for example, he altered the indication of tempo, and sometimes even the time. 'Der Vater mit dem Kind' was commenced in six-eight time as though it were a cradle song, but Schubert discarded this interpretation and turned the music to *alla-breve* time as more suitable for the emotional meditation of the father. There are also alterations in phrasing, an interesting example of which occurs in 'Fahrt zum Hades' at the word 'Cypressen'. The printed version has two crotchets on the second syllable and two on the third, but Stadler's copy phrases it as three notes plus one. It is unfortunate that the original manuscript is now lost for it would be of interest to know which really is the final version: the even phrasing certainly seems the more fitting.

A notable example of revision occurs in 'Leiden der Trennung'.[1] The climax occurs at 'zum Meer' but the tension is maintained to the end of the song by avoidance of any definite cadence and a continuous quaver move ment in the accompaniment. (See Example 5, page 34). The first rough copy ends abruptly at bar eighteen, thus: (Example 15).

[1] This song was commenced in 2/4 time, altered to common time, and finally to alla breve.

Ex. 15. Leiden der Trennung

The rhythm has been broken and a fresh section has been
started, but Schubert altered bars 1 and 2 of this so that
the treble continued the quaver movement and the bass
descended to G flat at the first half-bar: and then wrote
bars 3 and 4 in half-time so that the words 'Kam, aus
dem sie' occupied one bar on B flat, C, D and E flat, and
then carried on the movement from there. Merely by
this slight reaarrangement of material the song has been
lifted from heterogeneity to homogeneity. A somewhat
similar alteration was carried out in 'Die Wetterfahne',
for the nervous agitation of the fifth and sixth lines had

little movement in the first draft, in which they occupied
two bars only:

F Sharp	G

Er hatt es eher be|merken sollen des

G Sharp	A

Hauses aufgestecktes | Schild.

Here we have the gradual chromatic rise so appropriate
in a big song like 'Gruppe aus dem Tartarus' but out of
proportion in a shorter work, and the many semiquavers
necessary to get the words in two bars created confusion.
This was altered by repeating each bar of the accompaniment to form a four-bar phrase and so retain the
chromatic rise, and a melodic phrasing was provided for
the voice by introducing leaps of a diminished fifth on
the strong beats and appoggiaturas on the half beats, so
that here again we have a perfect unity brought about
by careful consideration of first thoughts which were
right in substance but not in form.

Hence we find that although Schubert had no com-
punction in abandoning a work that seemed unsatisfactory, and rewrote entire songs because the first settings
did not do justice to the poem (e.g. 'Am Flusse' in 1815,
superseded by the setting of 1822),[1] he also found that
inspired versions could be improved in detail. Not only
was the first part of 'Erstarrung' refashioned so that the
first stanza was repeated instead of only the third and
fourth lines, but the initial phrase was changed in order
to avoid anticipation of the mediant on the sixth

[1] See M. Brown, *Schubert*, p. 203. See also p. 128 for a remarkable alteration (of one note) in Op. 143.

syllable of 'Ich such' im Schnee vergebens'. The original
draft rose to the mediant on 'Schnee' but this was
altered so that 'Schnee ver—' came on the dominant and
upper tonic in order to transfer the melodic stress of the
upper mediant to the middle of 'vergebens' and therefore
change the thought from the snow to a state of mind.

It is worthy of remark that most of the alterations
were connected with form. Revision of harmony was very
rare and not necessary where the melody was adjusted
because that took place within the existing harmonic
structure, which was rarely, if ever, at fault. Only here
and there was it necessary to alter the equivalent of an
adjective or adverb in the harmonic grammar, to insert
an additional clause or delete a redundant phrase in
order that the song should be fully expressive and well-
shaped, for Schubert was fully aware, as the earlier chapters show, that without perfection of form it would be
unsatisfactory.

However there were some very definite problems
entailed in many of the poems he selected, but the fact
that he did select them is important, especially as he is
occasionally accused of thoughtlessness in this matter.
He himself said that he had discarded may poems he had
been urged to set to music, and returned some in which
he could find nothing poetic or useful for music.[1] His
choice was a reflection of his own nature, one characteristic of which was sociability. He was genial and obliging,
and if he had been less than a genius would have
produced only light music for the pleasure of his own

[1] See 'A new Schubert letter', *Music and Letters*, October, 1956,
p. 340.

social circle. The interests of his friends were largely extra-musical and the composer enjoyed with them all the varying moods of companionship and thought that arose in their meetings, readings and discussions. They partook of the springs of literature and kept the common human emotions of Schubert alive and alert, to be touched off in musical expression at the sight of suitable verse.

Much of the poetry of his period was romantic and this he accepted without question, but he treated it with an engaging innocence that brought out its fundamental value. He gave sincerity to the rather cloying sentiments of some of his material and an additional vigour to much more. He may be said to have infused a fresh atmosphere into music, for so many of his songs deal with the light and colour of the countryside. Even the tragic figures of the song-cycles and classical poems are closely related to, and expressed upon, a landscape portrayed with realism and colour by his use of illustrative material in melody and harmony. He was intensely responsive to everyday incidents and the delights of nature. The rustic serenade meant as much to him as the highest poetic aspirations, and the chirp of the cricket as the storm-tossed oaks, and whether it is a simple fisher-song or heroic defiance of the gods, whether the grief of an aged sexton or the cries of the damned in Tartarus, he was able to find expression for them all.

His range of emotions may not be greater than that of other composers but its various gradations are more perceptible in the songs, for no two are alike although they may be classified to a certain extent according to subject.

One such group is dealt with in the following chapter, not because death itself occupied Schubert's mind to any great extent—a glance at a list of the six hundred songs will show quite obviously that it did not—but for the reason that it supplies an insight into one facet of Schubert's thought. For a similar reason the succeeding chapter is devoted to the songs by one poet who exercised a considerable influence on the composer and supplied him with material which enabled him to express certain personal feelings outside the range of the other poets.

VIII

SONGS OF DEATH

THE mortality rate at the end of the eighteenth century was terribly high not so much because of war but on account of disease and pestilence, and now that we have largely overcome the latter causes it is rather difficult to realize how the subject of death must have been ever present in mind and therefore in art. As the antithesis of life it can never be ignored and apart from the natural pathos of the subject it has always been a means of dramatic chiaroscuro and the climax of tragedy. Even the genial Claudius dedicated his book to Freund Hain (with a frontispiece depicting a skeleton with his scythe); the care-free Spaun wrote the poems to two of Schubert's finest death songs, and the complacent Schober contributed 'Todesmusik'. In all the various cradle-songs by Schubert the poets cannot forbear from bringing in the last hours of the infant. Add to all this the religious aspect and the desire for eternal rest of those battered in life's storms or old and weary and forlorn, and it is not surprising that there are about fifty songs on the subject of death, excluding the ballads with a tragic conclusion.

The most easily accepted class is the personal lament, for although vigorous life may not wish to meditate on the subject, yet alone wish for an immediate demise, all have cause for sorrow at the loss of someone dear to them. One of the most moving songs in this class is the 'Grablied für die Mutter'. Both melody and harmony are simple. The tone is at first melancholy and subdued with one tiny outburst as father and son think how suddenly —'schnell, schnell'—their happiness has vanished. But their grief is assuaged as they think of Paradise, the healing thought being expressed by Schubert in his favourite method of modulating to the tonic major so that the mediant for the voice moves up a semitone. 'Ihr Grab' has not the tender pathos of the former song although it is more free in melody, harmony and form. Here again there is the heartbroken little outburst of woe at 'dort, dort'—there, there, she lies low. 'Bei dem Grabe meines Vaters' and 'Am Grabe Anselmos' are both solemn laments in very free rhythm. The former is in a major key for it is more in praise of the father, with a call for God's blessing for this 'good man', and a lament by the son that he cannot repay his father's care. The 'Grablied auf einen Soldaten' opens with a rather martial air and is inferior to 'Grablied' which is a beautiful expression of real loss, for in this the soldier is one of us whereas in the former he is more part of a military ritual.

In these and the other songs not mentioned there is nearly always the thought of future happiness and this is also the case in the other varieties of song on death. The setting for bass solo of 'Das Grab' and that difficult song for one voice—'Der Tod und das Mädchen'—both express fear of death but conclude on a hopeful note. To the Maiden death comes as a friend, but in 'Das Grab',

although each stanza also concludes in the major, it is
only in the last two that the poet expresses the thought
that death is a blessing in disguise.

The more contemplative songs of an elegiac character
are all beautiful. The most famous is 'Litanei', but Pope's
'Verklärung' is a very fine work. 'Das Zugenglöcklein'
is a longer and more involved composition but it is a
wonder that it has not achieved popularity. Towards the
end of the second stanza there is a swing to the flat
mediant and it closes in the tonic minor. In the third and
fifth stanzas there is the 'triad' swing—E flat, G flat; C
flat, A flat. The verbal repetitions vary. At first the last
two lines are repeated, but in stanza four the lines are,
1, 2, 3, 4, 5, 1, 2, 6, and in the next and last 1, 2, 3, 4,
5, 4, 5, 6. It is also noteworthy that each line is less than
one bar in length except for the last of each stanza
which is extended in order to make a full close on a
strong accent, and for the two lines after 'Ist's der
Frohen Einer':

> *Der die Freuden reiner*
> *Lieb'und Freundschaft teilt,*[1]

for whereas all the other bars end with a crotchet or
quaver rest, here 'reiner' is extended by a turn to run
on to 'Lieb'.

Compared with this song 'Todtengräberweise' is very
formal in spite of its many modulations. It is too square-
cut, and although the phrases are in four-bar lengths

[1] *Is he one delighted,*
Who in friendship plighted
Passes happy days

H

they have not the vitality and forward-urge of the short phrases of the previous song. It has a similarity to 'Don Gayseros' in outline and might be quoted to prove the authenticity of this song, on which some doubt has been cast.

The early song 'Auf einen Kirchhof' is a fine work but lacks unity. It has recitative sections with changes in time and tempo, but the last twenty bars are splendid in an outburst of faith. On the other hand 'Abendbilder' covers a wide field in perfect unity of form—the dewy evening, the scented air and songs of birds, the evening bell—the stars and moon—the churchyard, and then thoughts on the graves and the glorious resurrection. It opens in A minor and there are various appropriate modulations, but the whole of the last part from the address 'Ruht', o Traute!' is in A major. On the repetition of the phrase 'bis beim grossen Aufersteh'n' there is a major chord on the mediant which passes to B minor and then back to the tonic. In this song Schubert crosses the hands in the accompaniment at times, a device he did not often use. 'Die frühen Gräber' is a beautiful little song. It is in A minor with a tenderly turned cadence to B major at the end of the first sentence. The phrasing of the following passage especially at 'Eile nicht, bleib' ', is perfect here, but not for the other two stanzas. 'Die Sommernacht' is a brief tender meditation on 'das grab meiner Geliebten'.[1] It is all in recitative although the last few bars become more lyrical. The song opens in C major but the key is not disclosed until this last section in which the final cadence is prefaced by an augmented

[1] The grave of my beloved.

sixth resolving on the tonic. This song is akin to 'Trost an Elisa' which also is *recit*. Here again the key is vague and the only indication is in the final cadence in C major. It really commences in D minor, and six bars later there is a cadence in C major which passes immediately to the chord of B major. A little later there is another C major cadence, but no more till the last bar. This however does not deny unity to the song which is both expressive and impressive, but neither this nor the previous song will please those who look upon Schubert purely as a 'melodist'.

'Fahrt zum Hades' is in a class of its own. It conveys the terror of death and a somewhat similar thought to that expressed by Keats:

> When I have fears that I may cease to be
> Before my pen has glean'd my teeming brain,

It has been called a forgotten song, totally eclipsed by 'Tartarus',[1] but in power and originality of expression it should surely be ranked with the Heine songs. 'Tartarus' is a classical scene but this song is a true cry from the heart. It has individuality and the intense emotion aroused by the thought of leaving the beautiful earth and the knowledge so hardly gained.

The opening scene is vivid and the lament that 'da tönt kein Lied, da ist kein Freund',[2] first in C major and then in D minor is pitiful in the extreme. The change from D flat minor to A major is a terrific outburst of futile revolt ending in the melancholy cry of 'Wann,

[1] Capell, p. 136.
[2] There sounds no song, there is no friend.

Wann?' Then the opening is repeated with slight but impressive variations. The harmony is rich in passing chords in which the inner parts move in contrapuntal melody. In this more than in any other song the triplets for the right hand need careful study for the short phrases which may occur in any of the three parts.

Of the songs which welcome death one of the best of the early ones is 'Schwanengesang'. It is in strophic form and very expressive with a Neapolitan sixth cadence. Senn's 'Schwanengesang' is a most beautiful allegorical song which has never had proper acknowledgement for its ethereal quality and wonderful technique. The key fluctuates between A flat minor and major as representing death and resurrection, and makes use of the swinging triad in which the change is carried out with unusual discords and the use of first inversions. Thus A flat minor on 'Sterbegefühl' changes to what is in effect B major in the next bar with the perfect cadence in the next. The following bar is then in A flat major! The first stanza is in two-bar phrases: the next is in 3 + 1; and for this purpose the second two-bar phrase is 'telescoped' with slight variation so that with the first it forms the three bar phrase and thus ends also in C flat major (which is B). Then follows what seems to be the last line of the song in A flat major. The four bar prelude is then used as a coda, but above it floats what is in fact the last line, and the piano carries on for two more bars to close in the bass *ppp*.

'Der Jüngling und der Tod' is another beautiful song altogether neglected. (Example 16).

Ex. 16. Der Jüngling und der Tod

It is not only perfect in expression of the death-wish but is original in every phrase. The dying fall of 'O könnt'ich', the sequence of falling sixths at 'mit ihrem letzten Strahl entfliehen' with its alternating sevenths and six-four chords, and the phrases of the next two lines echoed on the piano with cross-accents portray the youth's anguish. Then follows the plea to death in C major (from E major) which concludes with a most moving cadence on the chords of A minor and D major, with the E passing to D by way of E flat. Death is then ushered in on a change from G major to the minor and he ends his solacing phrases in B flat. The song opens in C sharp minor and the difference between beginning and ending thus shows how the whole emotional content has been changed. 'Todtengräbers Heimwehe' is well known though seldom performed. Its sentiment has been scoffed at but it is a natural one for a toil-worn and very lonely old man. All his family and friends are gone and he wishes to rejoin them. Here he is now an alien—in the language of to-day a 'has-been'. 'Des Mädchens Klage' is different. It is the wail of youth which can suffer more bitterly than the aged, but the poet offers consolation in the last stanza.

This is brought out by Schubert in his first setting
(his second song) which is more in the form of a concert
aria with various changes of tempo and a recitative
section, and several lines are repeated. The second setting
of 1815 is the well-known strophic version which was
published in 1826 as Op. 58 No. 3. The introduction was
an afterthought and an inspired one. It sets the tone of
the poem with the triplets, the falling ninths and the
third chord which looks to be that of A flat (in the key
of C minor) but gives the feeling of a long appoggiatura
to a G that does not appear here but is in the opening
phrase of the first line.

The third setting, in 1816, does not make the same
immediate impression as the previous one, but familiarity
leads one to perceive that it is the more apt. It is more
simple but each phrase of the opening lines rises in
intensity. 'Es bricht sich die Welle mit Macht'[1] is
emphasized here as in both previous settings but is more
suitable for the following stanzas than the Op. 58 version, and the gradual rise by semitones is highly effective.

This upward movement in semitones where one
or more parts of the chord move so that there is
a gradual chromatic shift from one 'key' to another
is a favourite Schubertian method of accelerating the
emotion. Although so different from his sudden and
often violent modulations it yet produces the emotional
tension. In this song the bass rises chromatically from
G to C and above each note the chord changes twice.

In the second part of 'An den Tod' the same method
is used, for the bass rises from A sharp right up to F

[1] The waves break with force.

sharp, but the first three bars are treated sequentially in the melody with very beautiful effect. This strophic song has two stanzas of great power. The first is a plea to death to spare the young and tender, and in the second the poet cries for death to release him from his misery; and that two such diverse sentiments should have the same setting says much for Schubert's capacity for expression in the still early year of 1817. Contrasting with the 'sliding' harmony of the last half of the stanza, the first half has two powerful changes. It opens in B major which in the third bar suddenly crashes in to a dominant seventh on G natural to pass on to a close in C. Then fierce discords bring in B flat major, the bass of which changes to the A sharp mentioned at the beginning of the paragraph.

'Lied' ('Des Lebens Tag') is utterly different. It is a song in praise of death, opening in A minor with the introduction: (Example 17).

Ex. 17. Lied

Then follow two three-bar phrases in beautiful three part harmony, the first in the minor with the mediant in the voice part, thus accentuating the line 'des Todes Athem leicht und kuhl'.[1] This use of the mediant is then carried over to A major, and while the accompaniment makes much use of the arpeggio figure in the introduction the voice sings of the felicity of death with great tenderness and concludes with a brief reference to the opening bars, but in the major .

'Todesmusik' is in Schubert's grand style and has several of his most characteristic fingerprints, which have been mentioned elsewhere. In the section in F sharp major the key is not disclosed for seven bars and then there is a deceptive cadence so that a full close which really establishes the key comes only at the end of the passage, and this passes immediately to F sharp minor. A remarkable effect is achieved on the last page. There has been so much modulation in the course of the song that when, after 'allen Dingen' a brief interlude becomes chromatic another change is expected, but the passage sinks to a *ppp* in the same key again.

Of the songs in which death is implicit the two from the song-cycles are very beautiful and in both there is a suggestion of transcendental peace. In 'Des Baches Wiegenlied' it is the water that brings consolation, and in 'Das Wirtshaus' it is the bosom of the earth. In Mayrhofer's 'Schlaflied' a similar repose is implied. The lad lies on the grass 'an seine Mutter angeschmiegt'. To him as to the old minstrel in 'Nachtstück' the trees and the birds call, and he is set free from pain. In 'An die

[1] The breath of death is light and cool.

Freunde' the poet goes further and protests that sorrow and lament over his grave will disturb his final peace.

This connection of peace and security with death is a psychological manifestation which is expressed in several songs that are linked together by one of the few musical 'mottoes' which may be found in Schubert's works. It is not suggested that these were used consciously, but it is only natural that similar impulses should produce similar reactions. Such a case has already been noted in reference to the felicity of the mediant, but here we have a recognizable musical phrase. It occurred in 'Der Wanderer' in 1816, and was made the basis of the slow movement of the piano work which was later entitled the 'Wanderer' fantasia. An excellent case in support of the theory that the resemblance, although strong, was accidental has been stated,[1] and is supported by the fact that the first part of the theme is used in other songs in a way that we may be sure is accidental. It is a phrase expressing the deep melancholy due to world-weariness and the desire for the 'happy land'.

The first two bars of the 'Wanderer' theme consists of two elements. The harmony, in the minor, is tonic, dominant, tonic, subdominant and dominant. The melody remains on the tonic in the first bar except for the semiquavers, and rises up in the second bar so that the harmonies open out, because the subdominant chord is in its first inversion.

The song was written in October 1816, but the fantasia, which has a more simple melody (Example 18)

[1] *Schubert's Variations*, by M. E. J. Brown, p. 49.

Ex. 18. Der Wanderer

was composed in November 1822, but even as late as
October 1827 the song 'Vor meiner Wiege' opens with
the first part of the phrase in which the chords are
exactly reproduced and the melody is on the dominant
except for the one rising note. (Example 19).

Ex. 19. Vor meine Wiege

In *Der Jüngling und der Tod* (March 1817) the phrase is
complete except for the second tonic chord, and in the
same key (See Example 16) while the rising notes are
in the inner part of the treble.

The next example, from *Lied* of 1823 is more involved. The second and third chords are inverted although the dominant remains as the upper note even to the subdominant chord (See Example 17). There is also the inner arpeggio (mentioned on p. 112) but the resemblance to the original pattern is quite clear. Another case of the fifth of the scale suspended over the subdominant chord occurs in the prelude to 'Leiden der Trennung' (December 1816) where there is also a passing note in the bass (See Example 5) and in 'Der Blumen Schmerz' (1821) the dominant is also suspended in the accompanying figure (Example 20).

Ex. 20. Der Blumen Schmerz

At first sight these songs seem so varied in subject that it is necessary to search for the unifying emotion that caused one recognizable theme to arise quite unconsciously in Schubert's mind on each occasion. There is some connection between the wandering of the man and of the stream, and between the song in praise of death and the youth's appeal, but there seems little between the two pair of songs and none with a cradle or lamenting flowers. In 'Vor Meine Wiege' the sight of his cradle causes the poet to recollect his babyhood and the loving care with which his mother lulled him to rest, and he prays that he may be cared for as tenderly at his last long sleep. Here we have the association of infancy, mother-love and death. In 'Lied' the poet Stolberg personifies the earth as a mother: 'Mother Earth takes us all to her bosom. If we only look in her eyes we shall not be afraid to rest on her breast.' And in 'Des Blumen Schmerz' the flowers cry 'O, mother take us back again, for life is only pain'. This song has been generally condemned on account of the silly, sickly, sentimentality of the poem but such criticism takes the words at only face value.[1] A great deal of poetry is allegorical, and here the poet projects his grief on the flowers so that these are used merely in order to express his own longing for the peace symbolised by the bosom of the earth. None of the poets really wished to die; but they all proclaim a knowledge of a lost heaven, the unhappiness of life, and a longing to recover felicity, and it was this complex emotion that Schubert quite unconsciously sensed in their verse and used to express his own feelings on the subject.

The Wanderer and the brook come from the mountains which are a universal symbol of bliss—the Delectable Mountains of Bunyan, the abode of the gods. They descend into the dales, the vale of tears, the valley of the shadow. They seek comfort in the bosom of Mother Earth or the great waters. We are well aware of these emotional states of mind and when they are put before us in allegorical form we perceive the symbolism—often quite unconsciously—and are deeply moved by them. It is true that we are inclined to look on them with contempt as neurotic or hypochondriac, and pride ourselves

[1] Symposium, p. 176; Einstein, p. 252; Capell, p. 170.

on having more virile minds than these poets and
dreamers, but they are still in the unconscious mind
where they readily respond to artistic stimuli; and
occasionally break the barriers by which we keep them
submerged, as they do so easily with the poets and
musicians who are by their art at the beck and call of
their inspiration or unconscious promptings.

This emotional complex has its roots in extreme
infancy before and after birth when we develop at an
enormous rate, and the mind, although unconscious, is
forming patterns that cannot be erased. This period is
one of security and serenity. Other people shoulder our
cares and tend to our happiness. Mother-love is para-
mount and it is little wonder that in later life we still
retain the vision of a lost happy land and crave for it in
our moments of despair. Therefore the mother-complex
is stirred by any symbolic reference to a golden age of
felicity, to the loss of that state by the bludgeoning of
fate, and to the hope of regaining it by returning to
Mother Earth.

Now we see the fundamental connection between all
these songs. It is the desire for that felicity enjoyed before
we were capable of understanding its significance, and
any reference to it elicited a similar Schubertian response.
Thus fragments of the theme may be found in other
songs in which wandering is hopeless and aimless,
because the ties of love have been broken.[1] It begins 'Die

---

[1] Mr Hill wrote to me that during the war when so many
children were evacuated 'there were several who attended school
if anybody, even another pupil, accompanied them, but if one
went alone, he was found a long way off, not knowing why he
had wandered'.

Perle', the song of the searcher for love, and is more than hinted at in 'Pilgerweise', especially in the second line, and also in 'In der Ferne'. References are also found in such songs that mention the felicity of the grave, as for example 'Schutzgraber's Begehr' in the line 'Ich steige gern hinab'.[1] (Example 21).

Ex. 21. Schutzgräbers Begehr

This, like Example 5, has a passing note in the bass, but instead of the two outer C sharps in the second bar forming the dominant chord they proceed outwards to form a beautiful modulation to the major with the third in the voice. The song, which was written in the same month as the Fantasia, is most richly harmonized and phrased with great charm, the last stanza being in the tonic major and closing finally on a bare fifth, a very unusual last chord. Capell says that it is invalidated by 'something puerile in Schober's intention', but here again the symbolism is ignored. Schubert knew well the

[1] I descend gladly (into the grave).

'alt Gesetz, dem treibt mich's rastlos immer nachzu-
spuren'.[1] He ignored the world's golden net and its
prudent advice. He too was prepared to delve for the
treasure of his mind even though he dug his own grave.

[1] The elemental force that drives me restlessly to search (for
the unknown).

IX

SCHUBERT AND MAYRHOFER

MUCH has been written on the subject of Schubert's poets without proper consideration of the relationship between poetry and music, and it has therefore been generally accepted as axiomatic that the greatest poetry should produce the greatest songs. The poet's feelings have been ignored. He produces a self-sufficient work of art: a train of thought in verbal form that has a beauty and perfection of its own. He writes with the speaking voice at the normal rate of speech in mind. He produces the effects of *allegro* or *largo* by the rhythm of his vowels, and of *forte* and *piano* by the choice of con- sonants, and the more perfect his verse the more likely it is to suffer in a musical setting.

Poetry and music are separate spheres of art and when they coalesce the latter is always the dominant partner. A song is immortalized by its music and not by its verse which may be quite second-rate without anyone but the critic either knowing or caring. This is not to say that the selection of poor poetry is to be condoned, but it does suggest that what is considered second-rate may be first-rate for a song. What Schubert looked for in a poem was an expression of emotion or a vivid scene, or both combined, and that this emotion should be melodic- ally evocative and the scene be of such character that it could be musically expressed. Thus he ranged from moonlight serenity to raging storm, and from cradle-song to the agonized cry of death; and the ordinary person does not care whether the original was by Schiller or Schober.

In his adoration for Goethe Capell goes so far as to say that 'his brilliance, his brains, are seen to hoist Schubert up', and suggests that without the dozen or so great Goethe songs he would still be 'the beloved musician; but an altogether humbler figure'. Now although the loss would have been great it would not have made a great difference for we should still have the incomparable song-cycles and a host of other songs of pathos and power. Schubert's fame does not rest on any particular poet and some of his most loved songs are by authors who have no other claim to immortality than the verses enshrined in these works.

Mayrhofer occupies a place far above that. He had many an original thought expressed in felicitous lines. He has generally been misunderstood. Even in 1856 Bauernfeld wrote of him as half-forgotten, and his description of the poet as 'gruff, sickly and irritable' is often quoted while Kreissle's version of him as 'a cheerful, bright disposition of the soundest and healthiest sort' is forgotten. It has been said that the unhappy man was not a good poet'[1] and suggested that he dragged Schubert down into spheres of misery.[2] Let the songs speak for themselves. Of the forty-five poems eight are love-songs, nine are on classical subjects, four are long works, eight are personal expressions of which four only are deeply tragic, and the

[1] Capell, p. 21.
[2] Symposium, p. 177.

I

rest are lyrics of very varied character ranging from a jolly drinking song to the 'Schlaflied', and the boisterous 'Der Schiffer' to the serenity of 'Lied eines Schiffers'. About half the full total are great songs.

By the depth of his emotion and his love of nature Mayrhofer may claim kinship with his great English contemporaries. He was moved to personal expression by the lark as Keats was by the nightingale. As Memnon his sorrow sounds melodious to men so that 'vermuthen sie in mir ein selig Blühen', and then he repeats 'in mir' like that word 'forlorn' that brings Keats back to tragedy:

In mir, nach dem des Todes Arme langen[1]

and Schubert brings out the beauty of the first part and the intense pathos of the second just as he changes from the lively first stanza of *Sehnsucht* to

Nur du o sturmbewegte Seele, bist blüthenlos.[2]

Both poet and musician could range from the mighty heights of 'Fels auf Felsen hingewälzet' to consider the fragile 'Nachtviolen', or delight in the lingering raindrops after a storm. To Mayrhofer love of Nature was a religion. He saw himself as an atom in the universe. Enmity and dislike meant destruction but love and sympathy meant unity, and his tragedy was that he came to see more of the latter in nature than in mankind and yearned to attain unity with it in death. This thought is expressed in various songs either as a longing for death or in praise of it; such as 'Nachtstück' or

[1] *They think that in me a joy is glowing,*
  In me, who long for the arms of death.
[2] *Only thou, storm-tossed spirit, art blossomless.*

even the 'Schlaflied'. It is sometimes, like that of the Wanderer, a cry for a better but unknown land as in 'Aus Heliopolis' I and 'Am Strome'; or for pure dissolution so wonderfully expressed in 'Auflösung'. This dissolution is not for him annihilation; he, as Memnon, would be united with the 'Morgens Gottin' and

> *Aus Sphären edler Freiheit, reiner Liebe,*
> *Ein stiller bleicher Stern herab zu scheinen.*[1]

The thought of the stars is often with him: he himself is a solitary star:

> *Ich bin der Liebe treuer Stern,*
> *Sie halten sich von Liebe fern,*[2]

and thus disappointed in man he turns to Nature.

'Nachtviolen' is the most delicate of nature poems so wonderfully interpreted by Schubert. There is no reference to a 'sorrow and loss' that Robertson mentions, and to have turned the song into a love poem as Strangways and Wilson have done is surely vandalism. It has the subtle serenity of the true pantheist:

> *Selig ist es, sich versenken*
> *In dem sammtnen Blau,*

and

> *nun blüht in stummen Nächten*
> *Fort die heilige Verbindung.*[3]

[1] *From realms of noble freedom, pure affection,*
As a silent pallid star to shimmer.
[2] *Of love I am the trusty star,*
They hold themselves from love afar.
[3] *Blissful is it, sinking selfless*
In thy velvet blue.
And between us now there blossoms
Forth a mystical alliance.

It is more mystical than Wordsworth's 'To a Daisy',

> *With something of a grace*
> *Which love makes for thee.*

which concludes like Mayrhofer by claiming kinship
with a flower:

> *Thou breath'st with me in sun and air,*
> *Do thou as thou art wont, repair*
> *My heart with gladness, and a share*
> *Of thy meek nature!*

There are a number of happy songs such as 'Der
Alpenjäger' and 'Wie Ulfru fischt', and Mayrhofer sometimes points the moral of the poem as in the latter
song and in 'Beim Winde'; and in the beautiful
'Sternennächte' where the stars which seem to shine
so serenely cause him to consider our little planet
'Voll Misston und Gefährde'[1] and to conclude that even
we may shine serenely at a distance—a delicate fancy
enshrined in our proverb that 'Distance lends enchant-
ment'.

One of the most beautiful of all the songs is 'Der Sieg'.
There is no more felicitous passage in all Schubert than
the opening of this song which must be sung by a bass
in order to place the voice in the middle of the harmony,
especially at the close of the first stanza and in order to
get the low F on 'schlaf'. The harmonies are diatonic in
the first stanza, but the second is more modulatory and
closes on a *fz* chord of a seventh on D flat which changes
to a six-four chord on C sharp. This passes to the first

[1] Full of deceit and discord.

inversion of a seventh on A and then the bass falls to C natural as the bass of the dominant seventh to F in which key we return again to the opening stanza. It is a unique return to serenity.

As to the charge that the poet dragged the musician into unknown depths of misery, who, more than Schubert was likely to know the frustration expressed by Memnon—'Den Tag hindurch nur einmal mag ich sprechen'[1]—even although the force of his genius overcame the almost insurmountable obstacles that beset his early years; who more likely to experience that 'Boden, Idealen fremd, der trotzig deinen schönsten Träumen die rohe Kraft entegen stemmt',[2] when operatic rubbish reigned supreme, publishers were indifferent and even Goethe was too self-occupied to acknowledge the receipt of a gift from a fellow-genius.

Schubert could easily follow his friend's flights not only when he exclaimed passionately at his lack of recognition but also when he expressed the half-hidden thought of all artists that they are of the immortals. 'Ich nehme nicht, ich pflege nur zu geben'.[3] 'Wie blass der Mond, wie matt die Sterne, so lang ich kräftig mich bewege'.[4] Both poet and composer were ready to give with little expectation of return but in the light of their

---

[1] *Throughout the day but once may I speak.*

[2] *Soil, alien to ideals, that in spite of all thy fairest dreaming*
By callous strength frustrates thy toil.
(Schubert wrote of himself as a frustrated musician in
1818: Brown, p. 78).

[3] *I take nothing, I labour but for giving.*

[4] *How weak the moon and starry legions*
As power I wield in mighty orbit
(Freiwilliges Versinken)

work how pale was the rest of artistic Vienna! Only when they gave up their power would the lesser lights begin to shine.

If this is the message of 'Freiwilliges Versinken', so in 'Der zürnenden Diana' were the friends ready to welcome death in the hope of seeing perfect beauty, and indeed many a genius has sacrificed himself by the single-minded purpose with which he pursued his art. But do they not, at times, like Atys, sigh for a lost happiness? Yet the goddess is fickle and the sighs of the acolyte may bring dire consequences, and it was even thus that the poet foresaw his own end.

But although they both scaled the heights and plumbed the depths the poet could not easily forget the neglect of his contemporaries while Schubert's much more genial nature was ever hopeful as new fields of expression opened up before him. Although he set 'Einsamkeit' so splendidly his was too convivial a nature to subscribe fully to the conclusion of that poem. Nevertheless his inspiration enabled him to express the emotion with true feeling, and the lack of interest in this song by singers is truly lamentable. The fact is that we have got into the way of treating Schubert's songs as a kind of 'fine art' and handle them as though they were rare and fragile pieces of old china. We now require some robust and adventurous singers who will let themselves go on some of the songs, and a few of these Mayrhofer works would make for them a fine hunting ground. Such a song as 'Der zürnenden Diana' requires passion and power. It is marked *Feurig* and properly sung would be as successful as 'Erlkönig'.

Are works for contralto so numerous that 'Uraniens Flucht' should be unknown? Here is a highly dramatic work, and if Mayrhofer had written a libretto in this style it would have enabled Schubert to produce an opera that would have ranked with the greatest. There are lovely aria sections, big rising climaxes, passion and pathos; and the anger of Zeus is one of Schubert's grandest passages, especially at 'Er reisst den Blitz' when both singer and pianist can give, as is said, all they've got!

'Fragment aus dem Aeschylus' is a much shorter work but has the same power of expression and is a truly marvellous song, the cry for help in the storm being as awful as that of the boy in 'Erlkönig' although in quite a different context. Then there is 'Liedesend', the most compact of ballads. The first sentence opens in C minor and closes in C flat major. Then comes a passage of truly *feurig* rhythm and later follows a phrase, as the bard breaks his harp, of the trembling strings on an arpeggio mounting up on a minor ninth with the D natural ringing out in the treble against the D flat of the bass (the D being E double-flat).

Several interesting points in 'Orest auf Tauris' have already been mentioned. There is a starkness about the middle section as there is in 'Philoctet' for both are in barren lands, and the reference to 'Ceres milde Frucht' with the triplet figure faintly suggests the longing of 'Ganymed'. 'Der entsühnte Orest' is in such perfect contrast that one feels the two songs should always be sung together (if they are ever sung at all.) 'Triumph', cries Orestes on the surging sea shore, and here we have no rippling water, for the breakers roll in powerfully to his feet.

The song is in C and in the first eight bars Schubert makes his favourite semitone shift, swinging from C to B (major) and back again. In the following lyrical section the leap of a major sixth up to the mediant is prominent, and the song concludes in martial strains, as does *Iphigenia* as she too thinks of her future honour.

'Atys' has an underlying significance which is that an endeavour to destroy the ties of our own natural development is not only impossible but fatal. Atys among the Gods still longs for the homeland of his childhood. Dickens's 'Haunted Man' was cursed with loss of memory but Atys's affliction is caused by too strong a desire to return to his 'homeland', and his only means of return is by death. Such sentiments evoked some very original music. It expresses yearning, excitement and tragedy but there is little human warmth in it, except when Atys expresses longing for home and finally exclaims 'O wär' ich jenseits der Wellen!'[1]

The poem ends as abruptly as 'Erlkönig' but the song itself does not, for after the cadence at the end of the last line Schubert writes his longest postlude, which is in effect a transfiguration for it quotes the phrases of Atys's last cry—mostly in the minor but with a touch of hope here and there on a major chord. Here the music carries on from the verbal climax and adds what is beyond the power of words to express without weakening the effect of the final lines. A similar use of this power of music has already been cited with regard to

[1] *'O were I over the water'.*

'Die abgeblühte Linde', and among many other such examples 'Auflösung' should be specially noted. In this song the continuous tremolo bass which rarely leaves the tonic gives a stability to the soaring arpeggios of the right hand and the voice and conveys the feeling that in spite of the greatest changes the universe is indeed a unity. There is an underlying power from which we spring and to which we revert but all change is the outward expression of one universal force from which we crystallise and into which we dissolve. Such was Mayrhofer's philosophy and thus did Schubert interpret it.

There seems little doubt that the poet was more sensitive to general conditions than most of the Schubert circle. He felt more clearly the decay and corruption of society that were so soon to lead to the revolutions of 1848. Such dialectic struggles in society affect men very differently. Many seem able to pursue their ways with unconcern, some take up the challenge of the future boldly, some retire into their ivory castles or look back with longing instead of forward with hope. Mayrhofer had become one of the latter type and expressed his yearning for the 'peace that passeth all understanding' in some of the songs already mentioned. His sentiments with regard to civilization he expressed in 'Auf der Donau', and although as 'Der Schiffer' he could boldly defy the wind and storm on the great river and rejoice in a 'himmlische Lust', yet in the small boat on the Danube he could see only ruin and decay.

This is a song of great beauty and interest and although it commences in E flat major the depression is evident in the appoggiaturas at the half bars, and the voice enters with a three-bar phrase above the two-bar phrases of the accompaniment. The placidity gives way to nervous tension in the second stanza and here we get an entirely new version of Schubert's descending bass which moves slowly by semitones from G down to C sharp. After an impressive silent bar the opening melody appears again, not only in the minor but a minor third higher. This also leads to a passage with a semitone descending bass, but whereas the first covers eight bars here it occupies two only and is repeated between the final phrases in a most impressive coda.

Two other important songs, 'Fahrt zum Hades' and 'An die Freunde' have been discussed in previous chapters (pp. 107 and 82) and the few that have not been mentioned are yet interesting in a lesser degree. We have therefore in these songs a valuable cross-section of Schubert's interpretive music and what may be called a closed circuit of highly individual expression, for as Bauer has pointed out he seems to have a distinctive style for each of the poets, and certainly Mayrhofer was one of the most highly individual of them all.

X

SCHWANENGESANG

HAVING commenced this analysis with the earliest songs it seems only right to conclude with the last group even although some of the numbers have been already discussed under various headings. Many composers have their three periods, for their works may be divided into early, middle and late styles. There is never a clear line of demarcation for inspiration works at various levels throughout the whole of an artist's productive period. Even in Schubert's songs we find the early works which are to a certain extent experimental and exploratory, and although similar works occur at intervals in later years the main output quickly became perfect in expression and was brought to a wonderful conclusion by a group of songs which surpass even the great works of this long middle period.

The main bulk of the songs is marked by a vigour expressed in bold outline and brilliant colour. Emotions are not recollected in tranquillity but entered into with zest and put on paper with flying pen and eager anticipation. One feels in the music the joy with which Schubert seized on each new subject, and even the most pathetic of them have something of this quality. Now and then we come across a work that seems to be of another world, and a few of these have already been mentioned, but when we arrive at the last songs this different psychological approach is more clearly evident.

Although *Schwanengesang* is not a song-cycle it is endeared to us as a comprehensive group, and even though there is no necessity to perform it as such, the true Schubertian will always look on it as a unit and regret that some of the numbers are so neglected. They are not different from the main body of songs in power and beauty but in an increased tensity of form and expression which carries us into new spheres of perceptivity. Their range of subject is vast but in each there is that quality which Wordsworth indicated in his famous definition. Schubert had reached the summit of Parnassus and could look on the joy and suffering of humanity with great tenderness, and view the inner emotions of the heart with still greater clarity, so expressing them with an artistic detachment that produces an even greater intimacy than that of the previous songs.

Exuberance is distilled into a subtle essence, the apparent simplicity of which stirs the mind more deeply than ever before. The artist's means of expression have become by a kind of inner heat more elemental and penetrative and a new ecstatic quality emerges. As C. E. Montague wrote so aptly about great verse: 'You feel as if new doors of understanding and delight were beginning to open around you. Some sort of mysterious liberation or empowerment seems to be approaching'. Hence arises the paradoxical situation that the songs, so eminently satisfying, carry an intimation of still further purport. They not only throw the already known into brilliant relief but project a beam of light into the dim vistas of the still unknown.

This kind of art is difficult to discuss and impossible to analyse, and yet these songs cannot be passed by without remark even if only to point out the use of Schubert's methods in new ways. The melody is as tuneful as ever, flowing onward in delight in the happy songs, but more terse and pregnant than ever in the tragic ones. The harmony, still very free, is yet more trenchant and close-knit, and the form is perfection itself. There is still the leisurely flowing harmony in the first, seventh, and last songs, but one factor producing the high pressure of the others is to be found in the altered rate of harmonic progression. Where a reduced pressure would result from resolving discords in the normal way these resolutions are eliminated as one would cut out a resistance from an electric circuit, but in other cases what are usually mere passing chords become of the utmost importance. The result is that with these new values an unusual effect is attained by the musical equivalents of ellipsis and hyperbole.

One instance of the former is to be found in the introduction to 'Der Atlas' where half the tonic chord remains in the upper part although the bass moves to dominant harmony in bars two and three. A powerful example of the latter method occurs in 'In der Ferne' at 'Hassenden', which is on a B flat chord although the song is in B minor. If the bar before this had carried on the movement of the previous phrase there would have been a progression like Example 22.

Ex. 22. In der Ferne

and the B minor chord would have glided to that on the G sharp via the B flat chord. Such passages occur frequently in the songs, but here Schubert not only prolongs the chord but reiterates it so that it becomes the great climax of the stanza.

The Heine songs are the most remarkable for their simplicity. 'Der Atlas' gains tremendously as a song by the recapitulation of the opening lines, especially as it is a condensed version. This reprise commences a bar later over the accompaniment and hence with a different melody, and does not coincide with the first part until five bars later. Then a previous bar rest is omitted and instead of the third and fourth lines being repeated over the bass G and G sharp, the second line is repeated over G and A flat to keep within the original key. This produces a great power by condensation for whereas in the first part the voice sings with the bass on the G and G sharp and then ascends the scale in the next bar to top F sharp, at the conclusion the voice rises an octave in arpeggio over the G and thus reaches the climactic note—now A flat—in the next bar.

There is a similar economy of means in 'Die Stadt' which is also in ternary form although there are no verbal repetitions as the poem has three stanzas. The

accompaniment of the third is the same as the first
except for different spacing and the Neapolitan stress
on 'jene', but the melodic rhythm is altered and the use
of triplets brings out the sub-climax of 'Boden' and the
cry of despair in the last phrase. The final lines of other
songs are equally interesting because of the intense
expression achieved by the most simple means.

There is 'Am Meer' in which the two stanzas are alike
except for two bars, the first where 'unglücksel'ge Weib'
mounts up to top F above the pathetic A flat, and the
other in the last bar where what had been a half-close
on 'nieder' becomes a feminine full-close. In 'Der Doppelgänger' the final phrase 'in alter Zeit' with its extended
turn of phrase is clearly reminiscent, and how rightly
so, of 'auf demselben Platz'. Then there is the outstanding
example in which the opening phrase in the bass of
'Aufenthalt' is taken up by the voice in the last lines,
but the most interesting point in this song is the great
climax on 'starrender Fels'. The previous twelve bars
have been recapitulation and then up springs the voice
in a triple forte below what is in its context a clashing
discord. The climax seems so inevitable at this point and
so acceptable that one does not consider at first the word
on which it occurs. And then one realizes that this 'Fels'
dominates absolutely the mind of the man. Its inflexible,
staring presence acts on him like the basilisk. Here is no
'Fels auf Felsen' so inspiring in 'Aus Heliopolis', but a
crag like that implacable signpost of *Der Winterreise*,
and it suggests the most tragic possibilities.

The wonderful diversity of expression in this group
of songs, mentioned previously, is emphasised by some

striking contrasts. The sight of a mere shadow in 'Der Doppelgänger' produces a frightful outburst of woe, but contemplation of 'Ihr Bild' is expressed in a very simple but none the less significant melody with the most delicate nuances of minor, tonic major, and relative major. The differences between the big climax of the former song and the subdued tones of the latter, and that of the tender phrase 'auch meine Thränen flossen' (in 'Ihr Bild') and 'fliessen die Thränen' in 'Aufenthalt' cover a width of range in musical interpretation that it would seem impossible to surpass.

'Ständchen' is another marvel of simplicity in harmonic structure which carries on its intermingled major and minor chords a unique atmosphere of 'Liebesschmerz'. It is an expression of the ecstatic joy and pain of love rather than a mere serenade; an echo of 'der Töne süssen Klagen'[1] of the nightingale mentioned in the second stanza. Even the prelude suggests this in a subtle manner for although the first chord is D minor and the fourth its dominant the two inner harmonies belong to the key of F. There is once more the bass stepping down in thirds, but the chord in bar three is not, as one might expect, the subdominant, but a (suggested) ninth on the dominant of F which gives the following chord an ambiguous sense of being both the dominant of D minor and a major chord on the mediant of the relative major.

In the first vocal sentence these four bars are compressed into three in order to close on the tonic, but in the second the inverted chord on the B flat does really proceed to the dominant of the relative major, while in

[1] The sweet lamenting tones.

the final cadence it bursts out as a dominant ninth on A. Then in the last line there is the pathetic major—minor change of chord on D not followed by the subdominant or the Neapolitan sixth but by a rootless seventh leading to the dominant seventh of the tonic major. The whole scheme has in fact a wonderful clarity combined with a genius for avoiding the obvious.

This is the case also with 'Frühlingssehnsucht' in which the flying phrases in their sequences carry the ecstasy of spring's awakening clouded by the long sighing final cadences. The swiftly moving bass of the first sentence is followed by a dominant pedal over which the E flat of the cadence is delightfully suspended, and this progression sounds even more wonderful in the last stanza at 'wünschendes Herz' as the tonic minor changes to the flat mediant key. Here the fusion of dominant and tonic chords is similar to that noted in the opening of 'Der Atlas' but the two are poles apart in meaning.

The opening of 'Kriegers Ahnung' well illustrates the importance of the bass note in the diminished sevenths that form such an important feature of most of these songs. Here the bass of the C minor chords leads to the foreboding leap up to F, and this diminished seventh is followed by a seventh that is a form of the 'enhanced' dominant which does not resolve but leads by the progression to the tonic mentioned on p. 80. After the voice has entered there is a break away from this pattern, but it recurs at the end of the song with two slight but significant variations. First the bass F is approached more gently and then bars seven and eight of the introduction are reversed in order. The beautiful

K

passage commencing 'Bald ruh' ich wohl' is unusual for Schubert in its series of suspensions. It commences in C major and has a variant of the 'swinging' triad for in one chord the G is sharpened over a bass E although the note C is retained as an inner pedal, and two bars later there is a major third on A which here is really part of a dominant seventh to D minor, and then comes an unusual chord (C. A flat. D.F) in which the D is a suspension.

The serenely trotting cavalier of 'Abschied' is the complement of those galloping horsemen of earlier years, just as 'In der Ferne' is the summation (musically) of the many Wanderers: and 'Die Taubenpost' which is a song of praise to 'die Sehnsucht' is after all a fitting conclusion to six hundred songs that have so often expressed a longing for peace, or spring, or love, or even death. It is a felicitous work, the calm happiness of which is as fine an expression of Schubert's inner nature as could be wished for to close the journey of a very adventurous soul.

SONGS AND POETS

I T is difficult to state the exact number of Schubert's songs because the lists by various authorities differ according to whether or not certain groups (such as *Don Gayseros* and *Vier Refrain Lieder*) are counted as one work or as separate songs; lost and unfinished works are included; and versions with only slight variations are included with the final version. The total is also increased now and then by the discovery of lost works or altered settings. Maurice Brown's chronological list of all the works is the latest and the result of careful research, and provides the following figures.

	Songs	Total Works	
1810	—	1	
1811	4	6	
1812	2	21	
1813	6	66	
1814	25	34	
1815	143	189	
1816	110	168	
1817	64	90	Sonatas.
1818	14	34	Pfte. duets.
1819	22	40	Pfte. Quintet; Mass no. 5.
1820	18	25	Lazarus; Quartet Satz.
1821	12	25	Alfonso und Estrella.
1822	22	41	Symphony in B minor; Wanderer Fantasia.
1823	37	54	Fierrabras; Rosamunde; (Die Schöne Müllerin).

	Songs	Total Works	
1824	6	27	A minor Quartet; Octet; Pfte. duets.
1825	27	42	Pfte. Sonatas and Duets.
1826	24	41	G major Quartet; B flat Trio.
1827	38	63	E flat Trio; Pfte. Impromptus; (Die Winterreise).
1828	21	41	C major Sym.; Mass in E flat; String Quintet; 3 pfte. sonatas.

A few of the outstanding works of later years have been noted above as they account for the smaller number of songs in these periods.

The number of poets represented in these songs must be well over a hundred for we know of ninety-one and there are still 16 anonymous, who are to be found chiefly in the 1815–1817 period when Schubert was ready to seize on any likely poem regardless of its origin. For this reason also there are many poets represented by only one or two songs—the numbers being:

36 with one song

15 with two songs

7 with three songs

At the other end of the scale are:

Goethe	...	70 songs
Mayrhofer	...	47 songs
Müller	...	45 songs
Schiller	...	42 songs

These four poets had a great influence on Schubert, three of them for several years, and Müller in the two later peak years. The three favourite poets of the early years were Matthisson (26), Hölty (22), and Kosegarten (21). In the middle years there were F. Schlegel (21), Seidl (12), Schober (12), and Schulze (9). The interlinked influence of Goethe, Mayrhofer and Schiller may be shown in a graph if the number of their songs in each of the first eight volumes of the complete edition is taken, and the culminating periods will be more clearly observed, especially that of Mayrhofer as Goethe declined.

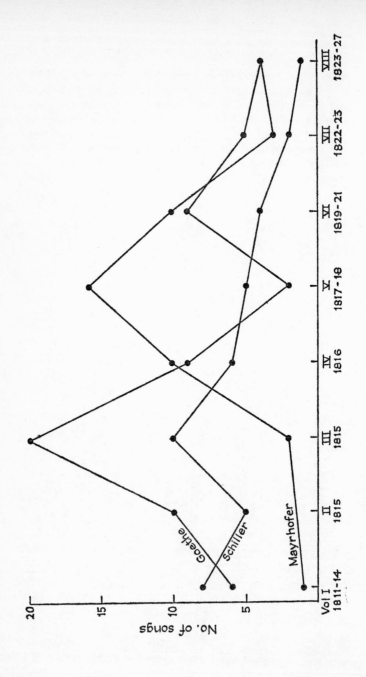

MUSICAL EXPRESSIONS

WORD endings may differ owing to grammatical inflection as all, alle, alles (all), but some alter as they do in English like sanft, sanfter, (soft, softer); schmerz, schmerzvoll, (sorrow, sorrowful).

Various prepositions etc., frequently occur, such as:

bis: up to
doch: yet
erst, ersten: first
ganz: all
hoch, höher: high, higher
in, im: in
immer: ever, constantly
leise, leiser: soft, softer
mehr: more
mit: with
nicht: not
noch: yet
sehr: very
und: and
von, vom: from
wie: as, like
zu, zum: to, to the

The speed indications are:
Langsam, langsamer: slow, slower
Mässig, gemässigt: moderate
Geschwind or schnell: fast, speedy; qualified by
etwas: somewhat, a little

ziemlich: rather (or suitable, proper) hence ziemlich lebhaft is suitable liveliness (see Der Musensohn)
They are combined in phrases such as:
nicht zu geschwind: not too fast
immer leiser und langsamer: ever softer and slower
Mässig geschwind: moderately fast

Abnehmend: reducing, decreasing
— allmählig: gradual reduction
Affekt: emotion, feeling, passion
— mit höchstem: greatest passion
— mit liebes: tender feeling
— steigendem: mounting passion
Andacht: devotion

143

Andächtig: devoutly

Anfangs, wie: as at the beginning

Angenehm: pleasant

Angst mit steigender: with mounting distress

Angstlich: anxiously

Anmuth: grace

Ausdruck: expression

Bedauernd: pitying

Behaglich: agreeable, cosy

Beinahe: almost

— die vorige Bewegung: almost the former tempo

Bewegt: moving

Bewegung: movement, agitation

Bewegung, in sanfter: in gentle motion

— in gehender: quicker movement

— mit steigender: rising agitation

— -wachsender: growing agitation

— unruhig: restless agitation

— mässige: moderate agitation

Declamirt: declaimed

Düster: gloomy

Eile, eilig: hurried

Empfindung: feeling

Entschlossen: determined, resolute

Ernst: earnest, serious

Erzählend: narrating

Feierlich: solemn

Feuer, mit: with ardour, fire

— doch nicht zu geschwind: with fire, but not too fast

Fröhlich: joyous, merry

Freudig: joyous

Frisch: gay, brisk

— doch nicht zu schnell: gay, but not too fast

Fromm: devout, pious

Froh und frei: gay and free

Gefühl, mit: with feeling

Gehend: moving (andante)

Grauen, mit: with dread

Heilig: sacred, holy

Heiter: serene, jovial

Herzlich: hearty, loving

Innig: fervent

Innigkeit, mit: with fervour, sincerity

Jubel, mit heiligem: with sacred jubilation

Klagend: lamenting

Kraft: power

Kraft, mit letzter: with utmost power

— aller: with full force
Kraftvoll: vigorously

Laune, guter: good humour
Lebhaft: lively, vivacious
Leidenschaft, mit: with passion
Lieblich: lovely, agreeable
Lustig: merry, jolly

Majestätisch: majestically
Majestät, mit: with majesty
Munter: brisk, cheerful
Muthig: spirited

Nachgehend: following

Ruhig: tranquil
Rührung, mit heiliger: with elevated emotion

Sanft: soft
Scherzhaft: jocose, jolly
Schleichend: moving softly
Schlusse, zum: to the end
Schmerzlich: painful
— er Erinnerung: painful remembrance
Schreitend: striding
Schwärmerisch: romantic, fanciful
Sehnsucht: longing
Stark: strong
Steigender: mounting
Stimme: voice
— mit leiserer: in light tone

Stürmische, desto: more agitated

Taktlos: without time
Tandelnd: playfully
Traurig, trauernd: melancholy, mournful
Takte, in: in time

Unruhig: restless
Unschuldig: innocently

Vertrauensvoll: confidently
vom Zeichen: from the sign

Wachsend: growing
Wehmuth, mit: with sadness
Wehmüthig: sadly
wie oben: as before
Wild: wild, fierce
Würde, mit: with dignity
— hoher: with greater dignity
— stille: with quiet dignity

Zart: tender
Zeitmasse, im, wachsend bis zum Haltung: increasing in tempo to the end
— -e, im ersten: tempo primo
Zögernd: lingering
Zurückhaltend: holding back

INDEX OF SONG TITLES

GENERAL INDEX

Mordent, 87
Mozart, 6
Musical terms, 84

P

Palgrave, 29
Pedal, 64
Phrasing contraction, 27, 108, 134
— expansion, 26, 129
Pritchard, T. C. L., 93

R

Rallentando, 83
Recitative, use of, 7, 10, 13, 16, 31
— number of songs with, 16
Reichardt, 4, 17, 18, 22
Repetition of words, *see* words
Robertson, A., 30, 116, 121, 123

S

Salieri, 46
Schiller, 3, 8, 121
Schober, 103, 118, 121
Schubert circle, 3
Schulz, 5, 19
Seventh—minor, 33, 36, 43, 47, 55, 64, 124
— diminished, 56, 64
Shaw, G. B., 40

Sixth, rising, 41
— augmented, 36, 51 64, 74, 80
— Neapolitan, 49, 77, 78, 80, 108, 135
— minor, 41
Song grouping, 11, 21
— Ternary, 15
Spaun, 4, 103
Strophic form, 14, 17
Symphony, C major, 96

T

Tempo, 85, 97
Third, major, 40, 55
— minor, 40
Tovey, 47
Trill, 88
Triad, major, 61
— chromatic, 61, 77
— modulation, 75
— swinging, 63, 71, 138
Turn, 88

W

Wagner, 1, 26, 51, 96
Words, treatment of, 9, 21, 85, 100
— selection of, 100, 120
— repetition of, 24, 27, 28
Wordsworth, 124, 132

Z

Zelter, 4, 18, 24
Zumsteeg, 4, 5, 7, 13, 84